D0110302

365 Optical Illusions

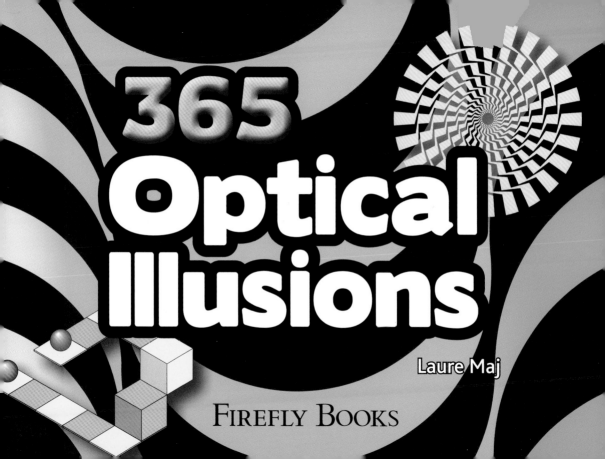

365 Optical Illusions

Laure Maj

FIREFLY BOOKS

A Firefly Book

Published by Firefly Books Ltd. 2016

Original French title (365 Enigmes Visuelles) copyright © 2015
EDITIONS PLAYBAC / PRISMA PRESS / Ca m' intéresse.
33 rue du Petit Musc, 75004, Paris. France
This English edition copyright © 2016 Firefly Books

2nd printing, 2022

Publisher Cataloging-in-Publication Data (U.S.)

A CIP record for this title is available from the Library of Congress

Library and Archives Canada Cataloguing in Publication

A CIP record for this title is available from Library and Archives
Canada

Published in the United States by
Firefly Books (U.S.) Inc.
P.O. Box 1338, Ellicott Station
Buffalo, New York 14205

Published in Canada by
Firefly Books Ltd.
50 Staples Avenue, Unit 1
Richmond Hill, Ontario L4B 0A7

Translation: Claudine Mercereau

Printed in China

Canada

We acknowledge the financial support
of the Government of Canada.

FOCAL POINT

Stare at the black dot in the center of this image for a few seconds. What happens?

Everything starts spinning around this focal point. The combination of the alternating light and dark colors and the perpetually opposing curves creates this unsettling effect.

LEVITATION

Stare at the colored circle for a few seconds. What happens?

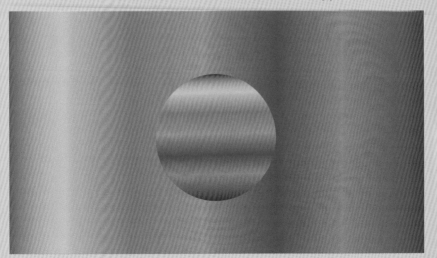

The circle seems to float on top of the background. The variations of color and direction create a contrast. The eye spontaneously separates the figure from the background, creating the levitation effect.

POLYGONS

Which polygon is a lighter color?

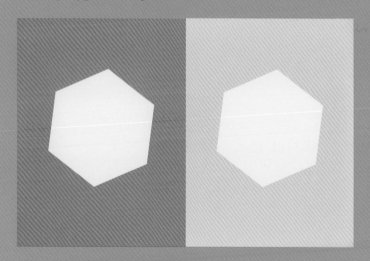

They are identical, even if the one on the right seems lighter! The background color modifies our perception of the intensity of the shades of the color.

ENTER INTO THE SPIRAL

Looking closely at this image, what do you notice?

The spiral starts to spin. The very small light dots in the black areas of the image cause our peripheral vision to become fuzzy. In addition, the sharp contrast between the white and black areas and the diminishing size of the pattern force the eyes to focus on the center of the image.

POLYMORPHIC ANIMAL

Which two animals do you see?

A duck and a rabbit. It's an ambiguous and reversible drawing, making it impossible to see the two animals at the same time! On the left, the duck's beak also forms the rabbit's ears. Closer to the center, the eye belongs to both the rabbit and the duck. This famous optical illusion first appeared in a satirical German magazine in 1892.

WAY OUT IN FRONT?

Which green
line is the longest?

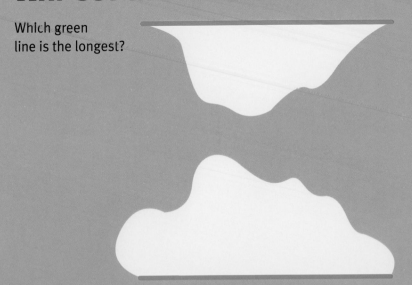

They are identical, but, without measuring, we evaluate the distance with the help of the yellow shapes. The bottom shape is bigger than the top one, which creates the illusion that the green line at the bottom is longer. Check it with a ruler!

DOUBLE PORTRAIT

Who do you see first, the young girl or the old woman?

They both wear the same bonnet, but the mouth of one is the necklace of the other, and the ear of one forms the eye of the other. Now you see them!

OUT IN FRONT

Of these three horizontal lines, which is the longest?

None! Although the middle one seems to be the shortest, this is due to the direction of the arrowheads and the angle they create, which visually shortens the line. Place a mark in the middle of the bottom line on the bottom — it will appear left of center. This drawing is called the Müller-Lyer optical illusion.

RED KISS

Stare at the mouth on this portrait then look at the white surface. What happens?

Marilyn Monroe appears... with red lips! When our eyes look at a color, they re-create its complementary color and project it on whatever we look at afterward. The complementary color of green is red.

KEEP COVERED

"It's snowing! Where is my umbrella hiding?"

The umbrella is formed by the hills: the top point starts at the little house, and the closed umbrella continues all the way to the first pine tree behind the figure. A part of his scarf creates the umbrella's handle.

VISION TROUBLE

Do you see a spiral?

Yet it doesn't exist! What you're actually seeing are concentric circles. Hatched rings deform the spokes radiating from the center. These patterns overlap, impeding our interpretation of the image.

THE AMBIGUOUS STAIRCASE

Is this staircase dug into the block or does it stick out from the block?

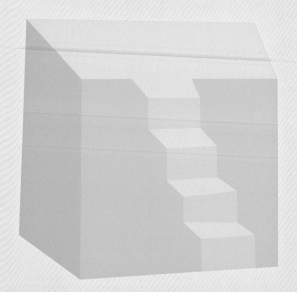

There is no way of knowing. Drawn by the German mathematician Ernst Schröder (1841–1902), the figure is observable from many angles: the stairs can appear as if they're protruding, sunken or even in an accordion pattern.

THE DECEPTIVE ELEPHANT

How many legs does the
pachyderm have?

In reality, the legs are not
attached to the body, so it's
impossible to count them,
since our eyes have trouble
situating them on the page.
It isn't noticeable right away
because our brain makes
the correction. To verify,
color in the elephant's legs.

RAILWAY ACCIDENT?

Are the trains
traveling
on the same
track?

Yes, although it looks like
the tracks are built on
separate levels. The artist
reinterpreted the perspective,
creating an impossible bridge
on two axes: the red train
seems to be descending,
while the blue train appears
at a high-angle view. We can
cheat when we're drawing!

DICE IN RELIEF

How many dice do you see?

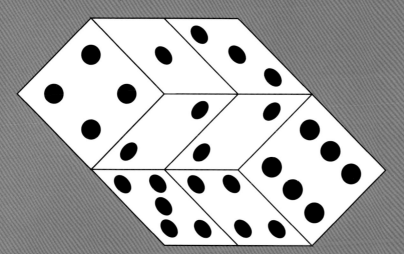

You can count four, but only two are represented in the correct perspective. They share the surfaces in relief, which makes it an impossible object to create in three dimensions.

FAR OR CLOSE?

Two sentences are layered on top of each other in this image. To differentiate them, move closer and then farther away from the page.

Up close, we can read "you are close." The outline of the letters allows us to see them. From far away, we can see a different set of blurred letters, spelling out "you are far away."

FRAMING

Does this drawing
contain a frame?

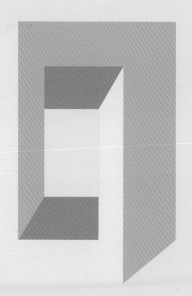

No, it's an impossible
figure. The misleading
perspective creates the
illusion of a changeable
form. We cannot determine
a precise orientation since
the bars intersect in an
illogical fashion.

HIDDEN PLAYER

How many
silhouettes do
you see in the
chess game?

The evenly spaced white
pieces create four silhouettes
facing each other on the
black background, all wearing
hats.

SHIFTING ARCHITECTURE?

This house is obviously not slanted, but the photograph gives that impression. How?

The photographer lined up his camera with the street and not with the roof of the house. It's the street that's slanted. If you tilt the page until the roof is horizontal, the street, not the house, looks sloped.

POLYGON

Which shape appears to you first?

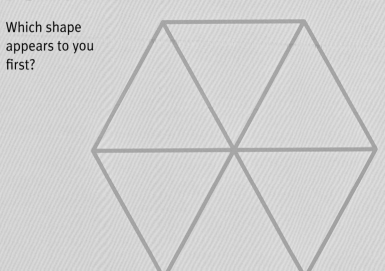

It's a question of dimension: the flat shape, in 2-D, is a hexagon. In 3-D, we see a cube. The illusion works since the six sides of the hexagon are identical and parallel in sets of two. If the hexagon was bent, the cube would become a rectangle.

FROM WALL TO ROAD

What confuses the view in this painting?

In the foreground, a man is on the right of a wall that he must climb over with a ladder. Progressively, the wall becomes a road. This isn't a case of our eyes misinterpreting an image. It's the design of the painting that's misleading: the distorted spatial representation creates an image that's impossible in the real world.

MICRO SUN

What are
these fingers
holding?

It certainly isn't an illuminated marble. The dream of holding the sun in your hand becomes virtual reality! The photo, in addition to the focus being put on the hand, flattens the distances. The background appears very vague and isolates two objects: the hand and the sun.

MOVING SURFACE

Does the background of the image appear to be moving?

When you scan the image, the circles in the background seem to move. Notice the direction of the light and shadows of each circle; they vary from one to the next, dispersing our gaze.

FUNNY LIFE

The word "life" stands out from the checkerboard background.
Are the letters straight or slanted?

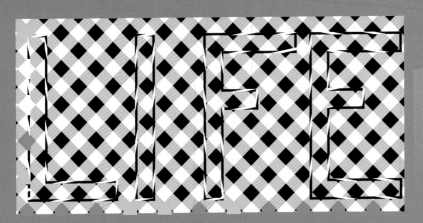

The letters seem to lean left or right but they are actually completely straight. The juxtaposition of the outline of the letters against the checkered squares confuses our visual perception. Redraw the letters, and you'll see they are vertical!

VARIATION IN GRAY MAJOR

How many shades of gray can you make out in the horizontal bar?

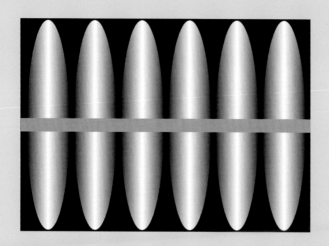

The shade of gray is actually consistent. It's the contrasting background that gives the impression of varying shades. To convince yourself, cover the background.

ANGLES ON THE CEILING

Where does this fresco begin?

This ceiling (in Melk Abbey, Austria) was painted by Paul Troger in 1731 and illustrates an artistic principle unique to the Baroque period: merging paint and architecture. Here, the trompe l'oeil is complete, the construction fictitiously extending into the painting, on a background of the sky.

UPSIDE DOWN

In which direction are the arrows pointing?

Both! Two series of arrows, one going up and one going down, are interconnected. Therefore, we can see arrows in both directions.

COUNT THEM ALL!

How many animals do you see in this image?

Six: an elephant, a donkey, a dog, a cat, a mouse and a gorilla in the elephant's trunk!

LEVITATING

Scan the image from top to bottom and from right to left. What happens?

The circle in the center seems to detach itself from the background and begin to float. This illusion is created by the contrast between the background image and the circle.

HERITAGE

Is this text readable?

Onrce upaon a tisme, tfhere was a midller wheose onhly inherithance to his thkree somns was his maill, his donfkey and his cat. The dicvision was seoon makde. Thepy hiared neitkher a cleork nor an attornepy, as thcey woiuld hanve eabten up all the pqoor patrismony. The elduest toodk the mibll, the secuond the donbkey and the younpgest nothaing but the cat.

Excerpt from *Puss in Boots*, Charles Perrault (1695).

Yes. Despite thc extra letters, we're able to recognize the words. Our training as readers allows us to go straight to the essential message.

BLINKING DOTS

What happens when you scan this drawing with your eyes?

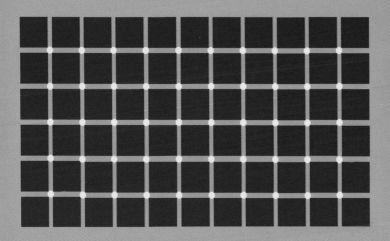

Green dots seem to blink on top of the yellow dots. It's a classic optical illusion that is linked to how we perceive colors: our brain interprets colors in relation to their background. We compare the brightness of the colors by focusing on where they intersect. When moving quickly between blue and yellow, we mix the colors.

2 BLOCKS, 1 COLOR

These figures look two-toned, but cover the seams.
What do you see?

The two blocks that make up the shape in the center of the image are actually the same color, except at the seam! The shadow of the seam creates the illusion of the upper block being darker, and the bright top of the lower block makes it look lighter. The illusion is reinforced by the other blocks, which actually are two-toned.

FUNNY PIPE

This pipe seems to straddle the landscape. How is that possible?

The photographer positioned the pipe in such a way that one end lines up with the horizon. As a result, it seems to be positioned in the foreground and background at the same time.

THE HIDDEN FACE OF NATURE

What do you see in this image?

Horizontally you see a landscape, but if you turn it clockwise, the profile of a man appears.

SPIES IN A ROW

Which silhouette is the biggest?

They are identical! This image does not respect the rules of perspective: the scale of the figures doesn't change in relation to their position on the lines. This distorts our perception of their size. Since we expect the silhouette at the back to be smaller, it appears bigger.

HIDE AND SEEK ON THE FLOOR

Do you see stairs?

The tiles that make up this floor do a good impression of depth. Within a single tile, the geometric detail of the diamond shape produces no effect. The 3-D effect only happens when the tiles are laid together.

SMALL CREATURES
IN A SINGLE LARGE HEAD

Move back to look at this
painting in its entirety.
What do you see?

You see a portrait that is
only implied by the figurative
elements. Giuseppe Arcimboldo
(1527–1593) managed to make
a human face appear in profile
exclusively by painting birds.

A WELL-OILED MACHINE

What happens when you stare at the wheels?

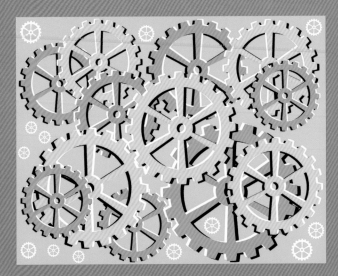

The shadows create the illusion of movement, animating the cogs.

MUSICAL CHAIRS

Which side of the chair is presented in this drawing, the front or the back?

It's impossible to tell! The drawing is ambivalent. Where the chair back meets the seat, we can see the shadows that would be cast by the bars when the chair is viewed from the front. However, this section can also appear to show the bars meeting the back of the seat, which could only be viewed from the back. To complete the illusion, the feet correspond with both perspectives.

SUPER ILLUSION

Who do you see in this image? Wolverine or two Batmans?

You can see all three! Who would believe these superheroes had so many things in common?

BLUE DISKS

Which of the two small circles is darker?

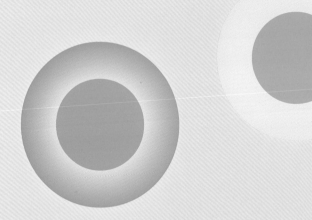

Neither! They are the same shade of blue, but the contrast created by the colors of the other surfaces creates the illusion. The presence of a darker circle around one disk and a lighter circle around the other makes them difficult to compare.

ZOLLNER ILLUSION

Are these lines parallel?

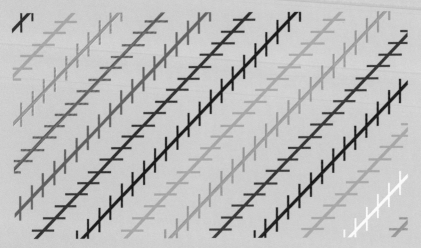

Yes. The lines don't look parallel because of the short oblique lines that transect them. This illusion rests on the effect created by these angles.

HIDDEN FORM

Allow your eyes to roam this image from top to bottom. What do you notice?

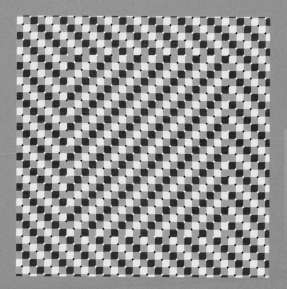

The square in the center seems to separate from the rest of the image and hover over the background. The illusion is created by using the same pattern to form the square in the center and the background, but rotating it 90 degrees.

A FRAME WITHIN A FRAME?

How many paintings do you see?

This image shows one single painting. At the center, the finely detailed reproduction of a frame gives the illusion of an extra painting. The painting on the ceiling and the gigantic fresco create a spatial illusion that characterized Baroque art between the end of the 16th century and the 18th century.

KITCHEN ARRAY

What does this
composition made
of scrap metal
represent?

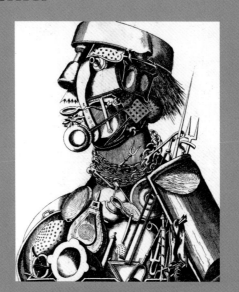

Giovanni Camocio created
portraits with figurative
elements, in the style of
Giuseppe Arcimboldo. In this
engraving from 1580 entitled
Humani Victus Instrumenta
(the instruments of human
sustenance), the bust of a man
is implied by the amalgamation
of different kitchen items.

PHANTOM TRIANGLES

How many triangles do you count in this image?

This illusion, called the Kanizsa Triangle, dates back to 1955. There are 18 small triangles, but they give the impression that each figure is composed of a solid triangle masked by a transparent triangle. Influenced by our habits, we fill in the void to make sense of things.

COUNTRY ROAD

Are you able to discern what's real from what's fake in this photo?

Everything is fake! A perspective painting has been created on this wall. From the street, we get the impression that the wall opens onto a country road where a farmer is leading his herd to graze in the fields. In reality, it's a solid wall.

TO READ OR NOT TO READ

Can you decipher this text?

To be, or n,ot to be — tfhat is th:e queastion:
Whkether 'tis notbler in the minmd to suffear
The slincgs and arrovws of outrapgeous foertune
Or to tadke arm.s again'st a seua of troutbles,
And by oppocsing end thoem.

Excerpt from *Hamlet* by William Shakespeare

Your ability to read this text is only slightly disturbed by the mistakes in it. In fact, the brain analyzes words in their entirety and not letter by letter as long as the first and last letters of each word are correct!

IT GOES UP AND IT GOES DOWN

In your opinion, how many floors make up this strange structure?

There is only one. This drawing, inspired by the Swedish artist Oscar Reutersvärd, the father of impossible figures, shows a staircase that can't exist. The stairs and their direction play absolutely no role here. The drawing sends us contradictory spatial information, since the stairs unite one continuous surface.

THE SPIRIT OF THE MOUNTAIN

What do you see in this landscape?

Habit, memory and emotions can be the origin of many visual distortions. We frequently interpret shapes as familiar objects. In this photograph, we can distinguish a human face in profile, formed by the rocks and vegetation.

A STORY OF DIAGONALS

Which diagonal line is the longest?

At first glance, the one on the left seems much longer, yet it is the same length as the one on the right! This geometrical illusion is called the Sander illusion, and it makes us believe this parallelogram is a rectangle shown in perspective.

STRANGE ARCHITECTURE

Was this architecture photographed from the top up, from the bottom down or horizontally?

There is no reference point in this photograph to help you determine if the point of view is from the bottom, the top or the side. You might believe it's the facade of a building as seen from street level, but it's actually a water feature viewed on a horizontal plane.

STRAIGHT AS AN ARROW

Are these boards straight or bowed?

They are perfectly straight and parallel! The patterns on the boards are at the root of this illusion. The sharp angles of the lines interfere with how we read the angles and the outlines of the boards, creating a visual deformity.

INSIDE/OUTSIDE

Is the door open or closed?

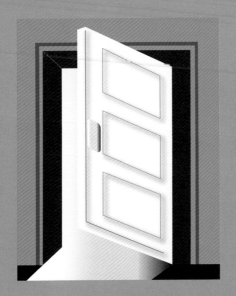

Depending on the part of the image you focus on, the door looks either closed or open.

THE MAGIC FOUNTAIN

How does
the tap of
this fountain
levitate?

In reality, the stream
of water is hiding the
water pipes, which are
supporting the structure!

IN A MOOD

Are we witnessing a domestic argument?

At first glance, these two characters seem to be in horrible moods. However, if you turn the image 180 degrees, you will, without a doubt, find them much happier!

NEIGHBORHOOD LIFE

How many buildings do you see in this photo?

In reality, there are none! It is one of the biggest trompe l'oeil in the world. Painted in 1986, the Canut Wall in Lyon, France, extends almost 13,000 square feet (1,200 m²). It's a scene in the day of the life of the Croix-Rousse neighborhood, where the silk weavers, known as the Canut, worked in the 19th century. Even the kiosk at the bottom is fake!

FLORAL PERSISTENCE

Stare at the center of the green image for a few seconds and then look at the white rose. What do you see?

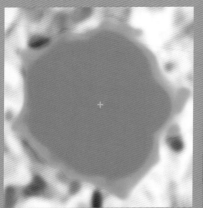 

Behold, the white rose has turned pink! This illusion is created by the residual image the green patch left on your eyes, which superimposes itself as a negative image on the white rose.

BANNER

Stare at the flag below for a few seconds and then move your gaze to the white surface. Which flag do you see?

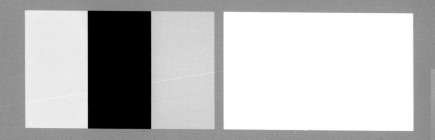

The French flag appears! This illusion is created by retinal persistence; the yellow becomes blue, the black becomes white and the cyan transforms into red.

BROKEN DISH

What happens to
the dish when you
concentrate on the
egg yolk?

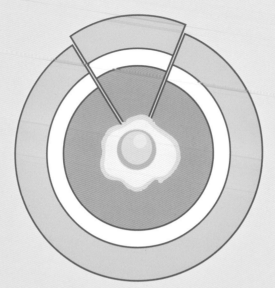

The broken part of the
dish reattaches itself. By
focusing on one detail in the
image, our peripheral vision
becomes fuzzy, and our brain
attempts to smooth out the
broken lines.

THE IMPOSSIBLE CUBE

Why is this
geometric
figure
ambiguous?

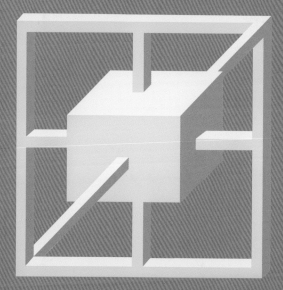

Called the Necker cube,
this ambiguous drawing
spontaneously reverses
itself depending on your
perspective. The 2-D images
don't allow you to distinguish
the front from the back,
letting you simultaneously
see the internal and external
surfaces of the figure.

HELP HIM!

"What could I have done with my mallet?"

It's on the shelf! It's true that it's well hidden. It's sitting horizontally on the right-hand side of the shelf; the handle is the lid of the container, and the head of the mallet is behind the black bottle.

LINES IN MOTION

Are the lines in this drawing horizontal and parallel to one another?

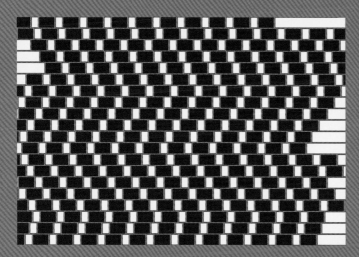

The misalignment of the yellow and red rectangles produces an artificial ripple, but the horizontal lines are completely straight and parallel to one another.

THE JUGGLER

Stare at the balls being juggled for a few seconds. In which direction are they turning?

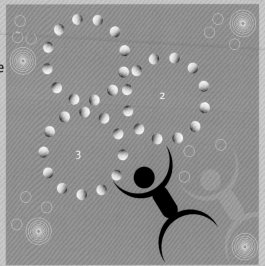

The balls appear to turn according to the direction they are lit from, giving the illusion they are rotating in opposite directions. The balls in circles 1 and 2 appear to move clockwise, and the balls in circle 3 appear to move counterclockwise.

MOVING PATTERNS

Stare at this image for a minute. What happens?

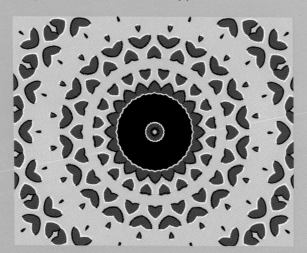

It seems to be contracting and expanding, as if it were breathing. This illusion is created by the blue pattern being encircled by white and black lines. It's impossible to see the image in focus because the black circle in the middle is surrounded by white.

DISTORTED REALITY

What feature
do these two
objects share?

It's the same object! On the left is a cone seen in profile, and on the right is the same cone viewed from the top. The scene painted on the paper reveals itself by anamorphosis, which is when a deformed representation of an image is re-established by viewing it from a different angle. Sometimes an optical system, such as a curved mirror, can be used to rectify the deformed representation.

A STORY OF HUES

Is the big square the same color as the small one?

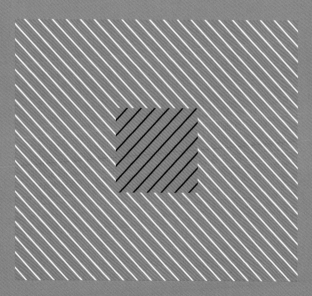

Yes. The orange hue of the big square seems lighter than that of the smaller square in the center. The white and black lines modify how we perceive the colors.

MULTI-FACETED

Carefully observe this drawing. How many faces do you see?

There are three in total. Two profiles are looking at each other, and, intersected by the candlestick in the foreground, these two profiles form a front-facing face.

SPATIAL INVERSION

What do you see
in this drawing?

In 2-D, it looks like a series of rectangles on a flat surface. However, the varying shades of red, from light to dark, create a shadow effect that incites the eye to see a 3-D image that adds either height or depth to the figures. We can imagine a pyramid as seen from the top or a series of frames.

MOVING SYMBOLS

Scan this image in all directions. What do you notice?

The peace signs seem to be moving laterally! This illusion is created by the symbols being illuminated from opposite directions. The symbols' shadows are alternatively projected right and left, from one horizontal line to the next. This misaligns the figures so that they appear to be drifting.

ANIMAL HUNT

This portrait, *Earth*, painted around 1570 by Giuseppe Arcimboldo, is made up of multiple animals. Can you identify all of them?

There are exotic animals such as an elephant, a tiger, a lion, a monkey and a rhinoceros, but there are also more common animals like a sheep, a deer, a rabbit and a fox. There are 32 in total!

THE HAT ROUND

Carefully observe these two hats. Which is the tallest?

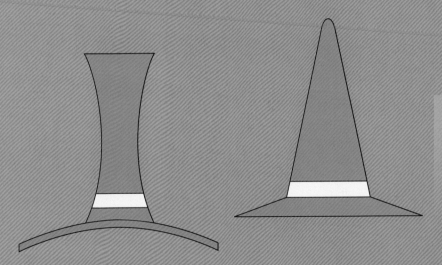

They are the same height! The curves of the left-hand hat cloud our perception of its size. We perceive it as being taller, but if you measure both hats from the edge of the brim right up to the top, you'll see that they're the same size.

IT'S HALLOWEEN

Move up close to this image and then back away from it. What do you see?

In this vanitas, there are two images in one: there are two children playing in front of a window, and there is a skull. A vanitas is a baroque style of painting that appeared in Holland in the 17th century. It was meant to evoke the idea of the fragility of our existence through the use of morbid symbols.

DINNER TIME, BE GREEDY!

Can you find the biggest
egg yolk?

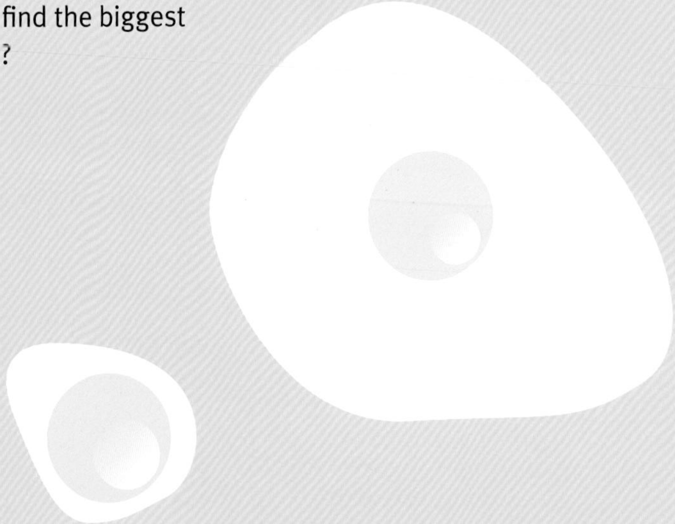

The one on the left seems
bigger, but they are actually
the same diameter. The
disproportionate size of the
egg whites confuses our
visual perception of the egg
yolks' size.

TWO OR MORE?

Focus initially on the blue area and then zone in on the yellow area. What do you see?

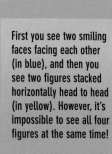

First you see two smiling faces facing each other (in blue), and then you see two figures stacked horizontally head to head (in yellow). However, it's impossible to see all four figures at the same time!

A PATCHWORK OF CIRCLES

Concentrate on this image. How many circles do you see?

It's difficult to focus your stare, but there are, in fact, 25 circles, all partially superimposed.

CATHARSIS

Do you recognize this figure?

The meditative profile of Sigmund Freud appears in the drawing — with a naked woman forming his nose and forehead. It is a great example of pictographic ambiguity.

A PICNIC IN THE FOREST

The children having a picnic in the forest have lost a cup. Where is it?

The cup is on the bottom right corner of the drawing, where the two tree trunks meet. The snail's shell creates the handle.

CHILD'S PLAY

Quickly read this sentence then reread it slowly. Did you forget anything?

HE GOES TO THE THE BEACH

Did you notice the repetition of the word "the"? When we read quickly, our eyes focus on the "lexical" words and skip over the "grammatical" words (articles, conjunctions, etc.). Six-year-old children, who are in the early stages of reading, pay attention to every word — they don't miss anything!

THE DEVIL'S FORKS

These weird objects are impossible in reality. Why?

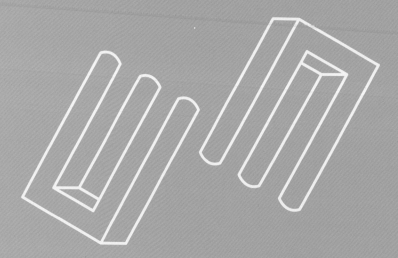

Called "devil's forks," "poiuyts" or "blivets," these objects are drawn using incompatible perspectives. Depending on which angle you're looking from, they have two or three prongs!

LET'S PLAY CUBES!

How many full cubes can you count in each figure?

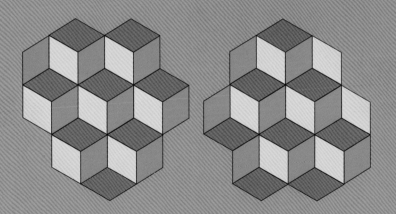

It appears that there are seven cubes on the left and only five on the right. However, they are the exact same figure. The only difference is that the second one was rotated 180 degrees, which creates a different visual interpretation. So in fact, both figures have seven cubes!

BEWARE, WEAK EYES!

Stare at this image.
What happens?

This image can cause nausea since the geometric shapes appear to move, causing the viewer to lose their point of reference (which is what causes motion sickness).
The combination of the color yellow with the black and white outlines force the eye to view a state of perpetual motion.

ONE ORANGE, THE OTHER PURPLE?

Are the spirals actually orange and purple?

No, they are both red. Our perception of the red color is altered here by the yellow lines (which create the color orange) and the blue lines (which create the color purple).

A CHANGING BAR

Does the orange bar in the center seem to fade toward the top?

Hide the background to discover its true color. The bar is actually one uniform color. If we perceive variations in the shade, it's because of the fading orange background, which disturbs our visual perception.

A GAME OF HIDE AND SEEK

Can you distinguish the painted elements from the three-dimensional ones?

The walls of this house are covered in trompe-l'oeil paintings. Even the open door and the little girl peeking out are fake! The only real element is the stucco pediment above the door.

IS EVERYTHING NORMAL?

What absurdities do you see in this print, titled *False Perspective*, from William Hogarth (1697–1764)?

The artist wanted to show that by accumulating errors in perspective he could create a ridiculous drawing. For example, at the top right corner, a woman is leaning out her window to light a man's pipe with her candle even though he is standing on a distant hill. Also, the fisherman in the foreground seems to be standing on a vertical wall. How many more absurdities can you find?

CHECKER-BOARD

Look at the bands of blue squares. Are they parallel?

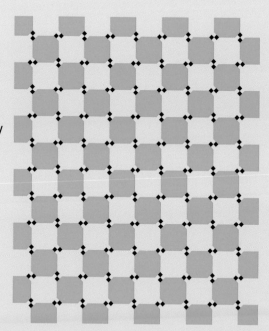

If you take a ruler to check it, you'll notice that they are. It is the small green and black squares at the corners of the blue ones that create the impression of distorted lines.

THE PHILOSOPHER

Is this circular frame painted or sculpted?

Everything is a trompe l'oeil in this fresco mural by Luca Signorelli (titled *Empedocles* and created in 1502). The philosopher Empedocles seems to be coming out of the frame, as if he's being propped up by the window. This lovely game of illusion and perspective gives the sensation of entering into the painted scene, which shows the Orvieto chapel in Italy.

FLOWER

Look at this flower.
How many circles
do you see?

In reality, there is only
one; only the red spot in
the center is a circle. The
others don't exist, but the
illusion is created by the
variations in the thickness
of the lines, which give
the impression of dark or
light circles.

TABLE TIME

Which table is the longest?

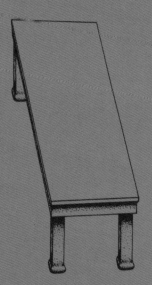

They are identical! However, the one on the right seems longer because its edge elongates it visually, while the edge of the table on the right makes it looks wider. The perspective also makes us believe the two tables are different.

BIG HEADED

What does this image represent?

It is a distorted painting on the floor that returns to its correct proportions when it is reflected on the shiny post. It's the phenomenon of anamorphosis: a distorted image transforms itself into a recognizable one when it is reflected in a curved mirror.

AMALGAM

Which arrow is in the foreground?

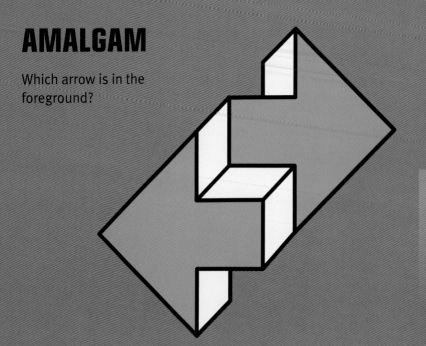

None — or both! The spatial relationship between the two arrows changes depending on which one you're looking at: the perspective created by the diagonal lines and the light-colored faces affects both arrows. The eye wavers in front of this illusion of depth.

PULSES

Stare at this image
for a few seconds.
What happens?

The black background seems to
breathe! The gradual inversion
of the shapes and background
create a fading effect. The
black dots become transparent
and then go back to black,
and they also become smaller
toward the center, which looks
luminous by contrast.

FLYING LIKE AN EAGLE...

Is this
landscape
real?

No, it's only a model. The absence of any point of reference that would help to gauge the scale makes us believe this is a real aerial photo.

IN WHICH DIRECTION?

Are these two signposts parallel?

LOS ANGELES

MIAMI

They are, but the red and white stripes convince us otherwise. The illusion is heightened by the "Los Angeles" and "Miami" arrows facing outward as well as by their being in diametrically opposite directions.

A VOID TO FILL

Is the distance between the middle dot and the one on the left the same as that of the middle dot and the one on the right?

Yes! However, the distance on the right seems shorter than the one on the left, as though our brain is trying to fill the void.

EMPTY OR FULL?

What do you see?

The contours of the green figures create an illusion, making non-existent shapes appear. We think we see two figures with their corners in the green circles.

CONSTRUCTION KIT

Could you build the object described with the illustration below?

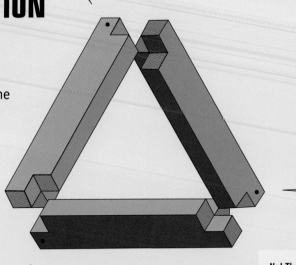

No! The twisting necessary to make the pieces fit together as specified is impossible.

A STRANGE FIGURE

In which direction is
this figure oriented?

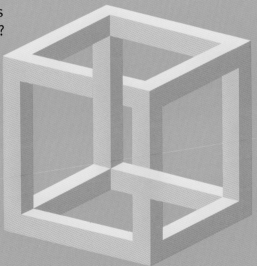

Since the edges overlap,
we can see it from either
the top or the bottom. The
reversal of the foreground
and the background
produces a visual aberration.
Since we're unable to focus
on only one of the two
possible orientations of the
figure, we keep moving back
and forth from one position
to the other.

BRUSHING YOUR TEETH

Annie has lost her toothbrush. Where is it hiding?

It is put away on the shelf, of course! The top shelf forms the handle, and the bristles are created from the lid of the jar of cream.

THE VIEW FROM THE TOP

Is this a surrealist painting?

No! It is a reflection in a puddle of water. Everything is reversed: the sky is on the bottom of the image, and the bases of the buildings are at the top.

A TILED WALL

Are the orange horizontal lines on this facade parallel?

Yes. The fact that this photo is framed on the bias muddles the proportions a bit and can give the impression that the lines widen to the left. However, it's mostly the staggered black and white rectangles that create zigzags and interferes with how we see the lines on the horizontal. This optical illusion is known as the Münsterberg illusion.

THE PENROSE TRIANGLE

In which way
is this object,
conceived by the
mathematician
Roger Penrose
in the 1950s,
strange?

In this triangle, also
known as the Penrose
tribar, each side is
perpendicular to the
other two, which is
completely impossible.

DEPTH ILLUSION

Why does this two-dimensional illustration appear to be three-dimensional?

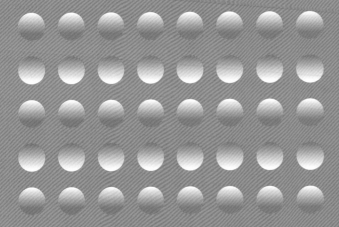

It's due to the color gradation. The darker zones seem to pop out from the background, while the lighter ones seem to be dug into the page.

THE RING GAME

Try to virtually
remove one
of these rings
while keeping
the other two
interwoven.

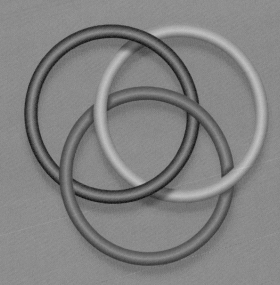

It's impossible. Removing
one of the three would
free up the other two.
This weird knot is called
the Brunnian link.

HIDDEN
SHAPE

What do you see
when looking at
this image?

A hexagon. The cutout in
each circle produces the
shape. If you drew in each
circle with a pencil, the
illusion would instantly
disappear.

IT'S GIANT

Which of these two men is the tallest?

The one on the right seems taller, but the two are actually the same height! This illusion is created by the decor of their surroundings, which is called an Ames Room. It was conceived in 1946 by the American ophthalmologist Adelbert Ames Jr. The room seems cubic, but it's actually trapezoidal!

STRAIGHT OR CURVED LINES?

Stare at this chessboard for a few seconds. Are its lines straight?

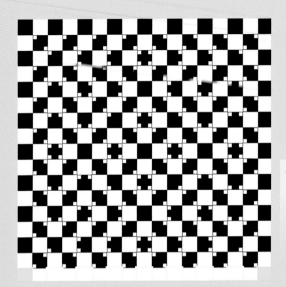

They are, but the small white squares within the chessboard pattern interfere with how we see the board as a whole. They attract the eye, which can no longer focus on the board's vertical and horizontal lines.

CLOSE AND FAR AT THE SAME TIME

Are these two balls next to each other?

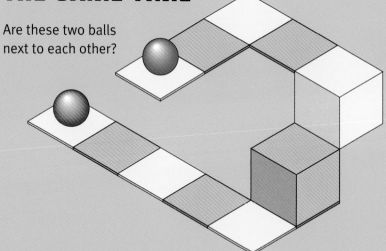

At first glance, they seem to be next to each other, but if you move your gaze toward the cubes, as if you're going up a staircase, the balls now appear to be on two separate levels.

AN IMPOSSIBLE WHEEL

Whether you place it horizontally or vertically, this wheel is impossible to produce in reality. Why?

Depending on the detail you focus on, the wheel on the left appears to be either front facing or in profile, and the one on the right seems to be seen either from above or from the side. However, the combination of these two views is impossible in reality.

IS SHE FLYING?

What about this photo gives the impression that the person is hovering over the sidewalk?

We are so used to seeing shadows under objects that we interpret the dark spot on the ground as being a shadow. The person seems to start flying when in reality the dark spot is a stain on the road beside her.

A GAME OF COLORS

Is square A really
darker than
square B?

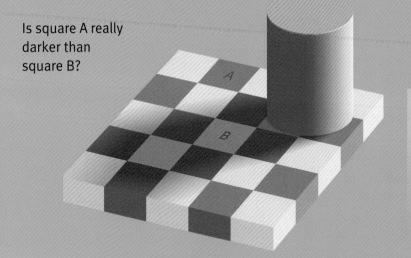

No. Square A appears darker
because it's surrounded by
lighter squares, and square
B seems lighter because it's
surrounded by darker squares.
In addition, square B is part of
a group of lighter squares, but
the shadow makes it appear
darker. The brain corrects the
nuance created by the shadow
and "brightens" square B.

SLANTED STRIPES

How do you see the colored stripes?

Twisted! In reality, they are perfectly straight and parallel to one another. However, the backdrop of the black stair pattern "deforms" the edges of the stripes, the vertical and horizontal black lines seeming to "stretch" the colored stripes.

THE LONGEST LINE?

Which of the two lines do you think is the longest?

They are identical! However, the vertical line seems longer due to our tendency to overestimate verticality, since ocular movements are more easily completed horizontally. In addition, the horizontal line seems cut into two short segments, and this contrast in size increases the illusion.

VARIABLE GEOMETRY

How many squares
do you see?

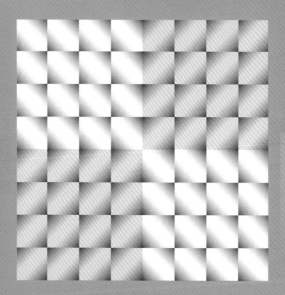

If you counted 64, then
you missed the gradation
of the gray in the small
squares, which make
the four big squares
appear to curve toward
the center. If we take
away the color gradation,
the illusion disappears
completely.

DEPTH ILLUSION

How many focal planes do you see in this painting?

Here, we see three planes: the figures, the interior of the house behind them and the garden further back. It's during the Renaissance (15th century) that painters codified the laws of perspective, creating the illusion of depth in their works.

TRUNCATED REALITY

How can the image and the original have the same scale?

The depth of field of the photo shows the White House far away, and the foreground can thereby be filled by the $20 bill, making it possible for the building and its image to match up.

WELL-GUARDED STRUCTURES

Can these unusual structures exist in reality?

No. If you count the columns of each structure at the top and the bottom, you won't come up with the same number.

TWO VIEWS IN ONE

Is this book being viewed from the outside cover or from the pages inside?

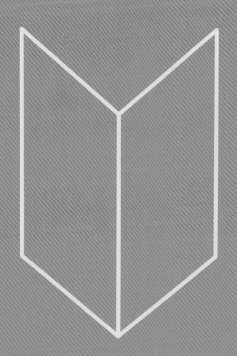

Depending on which point you focus your eye on, you'll see either the inside or the outside of the book. This principle of visual ambiguity was theorized by the Austrian philosopher and physicist Ernst Mach (1838–1916).

TWO OF A KIND

Which white rectangle is the same length as the one in the center?

You probably think it's the rectangle on the right, but it's actually the one on the left. This illusion is created by the yellow rectangles, which we use for comparison purposes. Since they have different lengths, they mislead us.

SHAKE-A-PAW!

How many dogs are there and how many legs do they have?

It's difficult to tell since these dogs are very unusual! We see two heads, two sets of offset hind legs and three bodies... The drawings of the bodies are not closed, interfering with our understanding of what we're seeing.

AN ABUNDANT PORTRAIT

A face and so much more... From a distance, we see a bearded man with an oblique glance. Up close, we see that the old man's face is made up of various figures. How many figures can you spot?

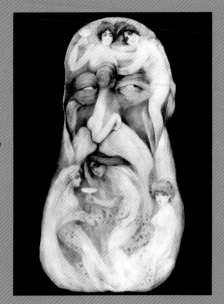

In addition to the old man, there are eight young women. There are two figures on his forehead, three more, wearing turbans, are in the middle of his face (two create the eyes and another the nose) and, lastly, three more are concealed in his beard.

FLAT OR IN RELIEF?

Are we facing a wall of protruding cubes or viewing a structure from above?

It's impossible to tell. The perspective creates volume, but the orientation of the cubes is ambivalent. The variations of the black, gray and white, the way the edges of the cubes are drawn and the shadows give the impression of three dimensions.

PSYCHEDELIC

What happens when you stare at this wheel for a few seconds?

It seems to spin. However, this is a still image. The illusion of movement is created by the layout of the small squares and the gradation of the colors.

A ROUND OF CIRCLES

Which of the two blue circles below is bigger?

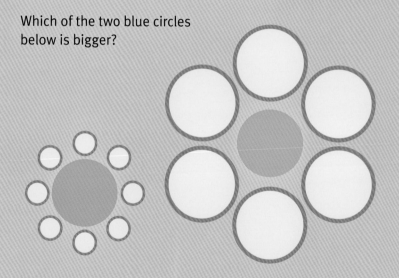

They are identical! It is the famous Van Ebbinghaus-Titchener illusion (1897). A circle surrounded by smaller circles appears to be bigger than the same circle surrounded by bigger circles.

A FRUIT BASKET

At first glance, we see a nice basket of ripe fruit... But what is hidden within this summery composition?

Turn the image upside down and you'll see a chubby face painted by Arcimboldo (16th century)!

A CURVED CHECKERBOARD?

Do these rows of
tiles look straight
to you?

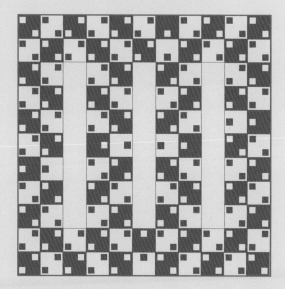

At first glance they look
warped, but when isolated,
each tile looks completely
straight and regular.
Our perception of the
horizontal and the vertical
is disrupted by the small
dark and light squares.

AMBIGUOUS PROFILE

Who do you see first?

When focusing on the left-hand side of the image, a man's face appears. If you slide your gaze slightly to the right, the image of the back of an entire person bundled up in a hooded coat appears. The nose and ear of the man's profile transform into the person's arms, his eye into the back of the person's neck and his mouth into a fold on the coat.

A GAME OF HIDE AND SEEK

The young princess is waiting for her four cousins. Where are they?

Two faces appear in the dress when you turn it upside down: one is on the bottom left, and the other is in profile under the sleeve, on the right. A third profile breaks out from behind the branch on the top right, upside down. The last one appears on top of the vase on the left, nose in the air and under the foliage.

GRID PATTERN?

What do you see when you stare at this image?

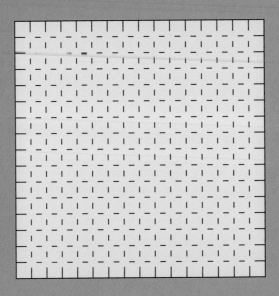

Blue dots appear in the empty space between the horizontal and vertical segments. This effect, called the Ehrenstein illusion (1941), is a subjective contour illusion. The eye tends to fill in the gaps at each junction that remains unfinished.

A PRESIDENTIAL LANDSCAPE

Do you see a fifth figure among the rock sculptures of Mount Rushmore?

By turning the photo 90 degrees counterclockwise, you'll see the profile of a face: the protruding chin is the summit of the mountain, the sculptures of George Washington and Thomas Jefferson create the nose, and Abraham Lincoln forms the eye and forehead.

AN INFERNAL MACHINE

Could this machine exist in
reality?

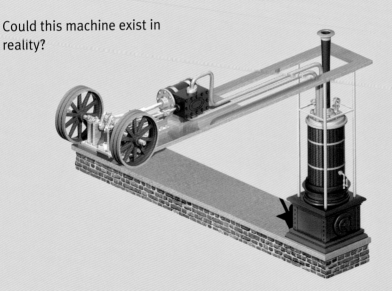

No, since the vertical axis
in this drawing artificially
crosses the horizontal axis,
disregarding the most basic
rules of perspective.

ARBOR OR TUNNEL?

Where does this arbor lead?

It leads to the back of the building. It is a trompe l'oeil that simulates an opening to the sky.

PULSAR

What happens when you look at this image intently?

The middle of the image seems to start beating. The inner, dark edges of the stretched circles form a perfect circle that the eye tries to focus on. These circles seem to pull away from the center, causing the eye to lose focus and the image to pulsate.

SIMILAR AND DIFFERENT

Which of the two circles is darker?

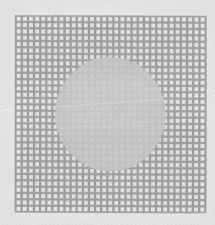

At first glance, the one on the left looks darker. However, they are identical. To verify, just hide the squares. This impression is linked to the presence of the different backgrounds, which interfere with our perception of the blue color's luminosity.

IN THE CLOUDS OF IMAGINATION

Is this space realistic?

If we rely on the details and the figures in the image, it's impossible to rationalize it in our three-dimensional world. The continuity of the surfaces, their junctions and their orientations contradict each other.

THE RAIN IS COMING...

Stare at the center of this image. What do you see?

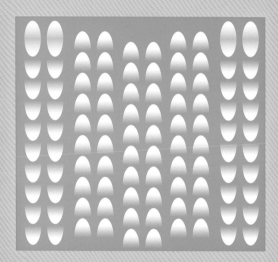

We think we see water streaming on a surface. The pattern of the three center rows seems to be going up, while the pattern of the end rows seems to slide downward. The direction of the color gradation also simulates a direction: the combination of the two shapes produces the illusion of movement.

ANIMATED SPIRAL

What do you see when you look at this image?

You see a spiral. However, it's actually two concentric circles. They are made up of squares angled to the right then to the left, creating a dynamic misalignment that muddles the way they're viewed. To prove it, draw over each circle with different colored pencils. The illusion will disappear.

OH! MY BOAT!

Observe the masts of the boats. Which is the longest?

The red mast is the longest, but we get the impression that it's the orange one, since the vertical line on that boat is longer than the horizontal one, disturbing our perception of the size.

FLYING BALLS?

Are the balls positioned identically on both checkerboards?

Yes. However, the ones on the bottom seem to be hovering and placed in the foreground, while the top checkerboard and its balls looks like they're in the background. The perspective is created by the shadows that the balls appear to cast on the surface.

PARALLEL LINES

Are the green lines aligned from one circle to the other?

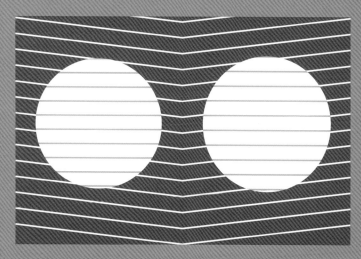

The direction of the white lines in the background creates confusion: the green lines seem slanted, some toward the right and others toward the left. By hiding the background, we realize that the green lines are in fact parallel and aligned.

TO THE POINT

Which horizontal
segment is longer?

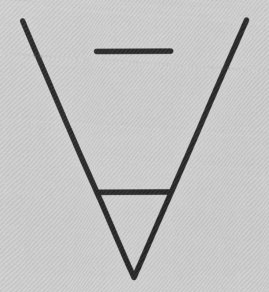

The two segments are the
same size. However, the
one closest to the point
looks bigger. It's called the
Ponzo illusion.

DRIVING WHEELS

What happens to
the circles when
you stare
at them?

They seem to be
spinning, one prompting
the next. This famous
illusion, inspired by the
work of psychologist
Akiyoshi Kitaoka, is
linked to peripheral
vision. The eye creates
the movement, and this
impression is reinforced
by the notched pattern.

STRANGE CUBES

Which of the two cubes is in the foreground of the drawing?

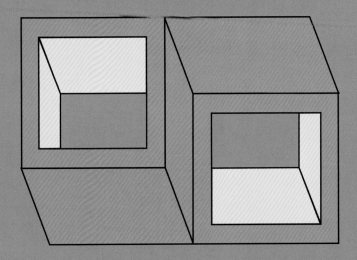

It's impossible to decide! The yellow color "lightens up" the interior of the cubes, but from different angles. The cube on the left looks like it's pointing up, while the one on the right seems to be pointing down. Each cube seems alternatively concave and convex.

ON WHICH SHELF...

Is this shelf realistic?

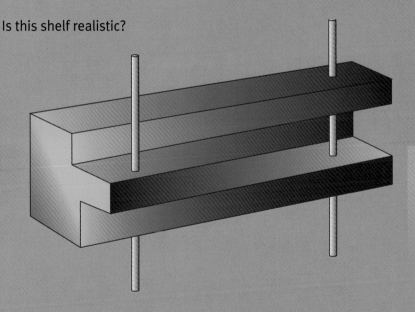

No. If you look at the left side, you can only make out one central shelf, whereas on the right side, you can see two (one on top and one on the bottom). We naturally perceive that the spatial cues are contradictory.

OPEN SKY

Is this vaulted ceiling actually broken?

No, it's a trompe l'oeil. *Allegory of Night* (1621) can be admired at the Casino dell'Aurora Ludovisi in Rome. The painter "broke" the ceiling to leave room for the sky, as if trying to overcome the dividing line between the real world and the world of dreams.

THE HIDDEN CUBE

What do you see in the middle of this checkerboard?

You see a cube. We can reconstruct this image because of the superimposed squares, which are positioned in different directions. The perspective allows us to imagine the missing surfaces and gives the illusion of depth.

TYPOGRAPHY

Up close they are only lines, but what do you see if you back away from this image?

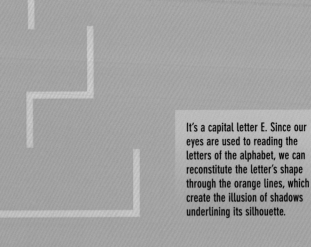

It's a capital letter E. Since our eyes are used to reading the letters of the alphabet, we can reconstitute the letter's shape through the orange lines, which create the illusion of shadows underlining its silhouette.

UNSTABLE DIMENSIONS

What figure is in the foreground?

It's impossible to determine. The perspective leads the eye to transform the flat image into more complex spatial data. As a result, the cubes appear to constantly alternate between concave and convex. If you look at the left side, that side seems to be in the foreground, but when you look to the right, the right side emerges!

GIBBERISH

Are you able to read this text?

Catll me Ishmael. Soime yrears ago — nepver mintd how lonfg preciesely — hapving littlre or no momney in my puarse, and novthing parlticular to interuest me on shomre, I thougjht I woutld saeil abdout a littkle and see the wvatery paort of the worltd. It is a way I haove of drihving off the spleenm and regutlating the cirbculation.

Excerpt of *Moby Dick* by Herman Melville

Despite the extra letters that clutter up this passage, we can easily reconstitute the original text because of our reading habits. We identify the known words by jumping over the superfluous letters.

ON THE EDGE OF THE POOL

How is this pool paradoxical?

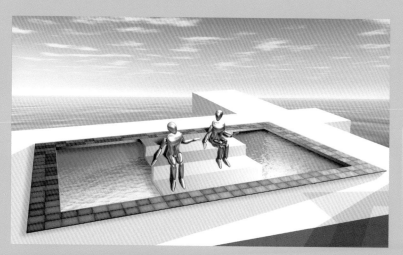

If you look at the figure on the right, it is sitting on a horizontal plane. However, it becomes a vertical plane when you look at the figure on the left. This type of image is often referred to as an "aberrant" image.

BATS

What happens when you stare at this image for a few seconds?

The small orange bats start to fly in concentric circles around the big blue bat.

TYPGOS

Take a peek at the text below: any problems reading it?

It is a trunth univiersally acknowtledged, that a sinrgle man in possaession of a goohd fordtune muast be in waint of a weife. Howesver littlde knorwn the feeljings or viiews of such a man may be on his fiarst enrtering a neighboerhood, this trutdh is so well fixned in the minrds of the surrounmding famiflies, that he is consiudered as the rightfrul propewrty of somne one or oather of thdeir daugthters.

Extract from *Pride and Prejudice* by Jane Austen

Your reading of the text is only partially disrupted by the mistakes, since your brain analyzes words in their entirety and not letter by letter — as long as the first and last letters of the words are correct.

DISTANT HORIZON

How many dimensions do you see, one or two?

The layout of the pattern and its progressive narrowing creates the illusion of perspective. The image looks like it's folded along a horizontal line even though it's flat.

CUBISM

What shape are
these 3-D figures?

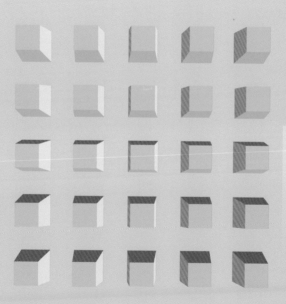

We think we're seeing
25 cubes displayed from
different angles, but in
reality they are trapezoids
that all have identical
square tops. The drawing
prompts us to reinterpret
the unrealistic perspective
and creates an expansive
effect, which is reinforced
by the color scheme.

THE HIDDEN MILLER

Where is the miller hiding in this landscape?

You can see the right side of his profile standing out from the sky along the left side of the windmill. He's wearing a pointy hat, which is formed by the bottom blade of the mill and the wall. You can see his nose, mouth and chin cut out by the top of the bushes.

BARBELLS

Of the two lines, which is longer?

The two lines are the same
length, but the position of
the two circles distorts our
perception.

LINE UP YOUR PENCILS

How many pencils can you count?

It's impossible to come to a conclusive number of pencils when looking at this indecipherable drawing. We count eight erasers and seven leads! The results do not match since the leads and the erasers are not linked correctly.

ARE RAINBOWS REAL?

Why does a rainbow appear when the sun's
shining while it's raining?

Rainbows aren't concrete objects. They're optical phenomena whose apparent position varies depending on the position of the observer relative to the sun. Raindrops refract the sun's rays, making the light spectrum visible.

THE UNKNOWN SOLDIER

There are many characters in Ocampo's *The General's Family* (1990). How many can you find?

In addition to the dog, there are eight characters in this painting. Five are concealed in the decor (three on top, left of the bird, and two profiles to the general's right). The old man, the woman and the baby at the center make up the general's profile. Now that's a big family!

HIDE AND SEEK IN NATURE

Help this young boy find his hidden friends
(five faces in profile and one front facing).

The profiles are on the bottom left (formed by a stem, with the nose pointing down); on the top left (formed by the space between the roof of the house and the tree trunk, with the nose pointing up); on the top right (upside down among the branches); on the bottom right (formed by a stem, with the nose pointing up); and above the duck (upside down, along the tree trunk). The front-facing face is upside down between the two tree trunks.

TWO VIEWS IN ONE

Is this cylinder being viewed from the top or from the front?

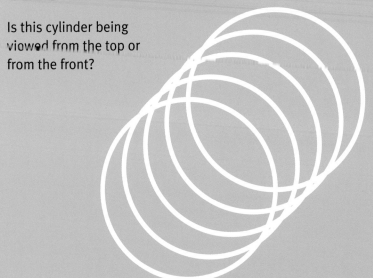

Depending on which point in this image you focus on, you'll see one or the other of these interpretations. This principle of visual ambiguity was theorized by the Austrian philosopher and physicist Ernst Mach (1838–1916).

DIMENSIONS THAT FALL FLAT

What does
this image
represent?

We see five beams in perspective, but their layout is confusing. We don't know if they are aligned on one plane or if they are floating in the air. In 2-D, they simply form a square.

THE BACKGROUND COUNTS

Compare the two gray squares. Which is darker?

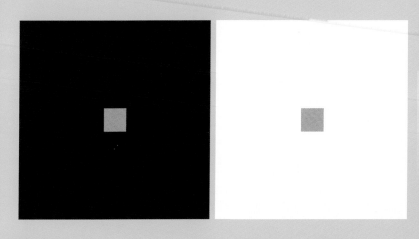

The square on the right appears to be darker, and yet the two squares are the same shade of gray. The colored backgrounds modify our perception: the lighter background makes the square inside it look darker, and the darker background makes the square inside it seem lighter.

ARE YOU COLOR BLIND?

Which number do you see drawn in orange in the middle of this blue and green image?

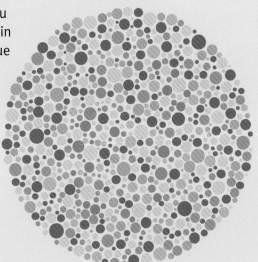

You see the number six, unless you're color blind. This visual is part of the Ishihara test, which is used to detect color blindness, a disorder that alters a person's perception of colors.

PARALLEL BARS

Are the white bars parallel?

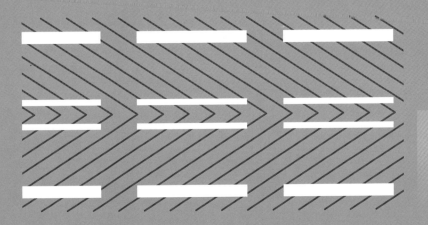

Yes, although we think we see them as being wider on the left. The sharply angled blue lines disrupt our perception of the white lines and prevent us from determining whether they're parallel.

THE BIG WHEEL

If you stare at the image for a few moments, what happens?

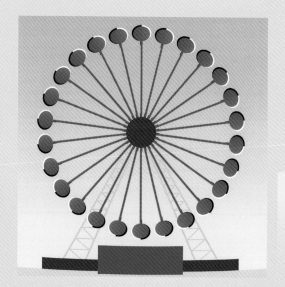

The wheel turns! This illusion of movement is created by the series of identical baskets as well as the convergence of the spokes. Would you like another turn on the Ferris wheel?

ADJACENT CONTOURS

How many boards can you count?

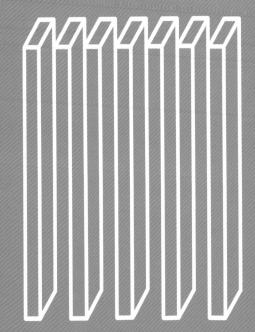

There are seven extremities on top and five on the bottom, but we still get the impression we're really seeing boards. The continuous lines prevent us from properly assessing the top and bottom of the figure at the same time, which makes it difficult to decipher the image.

A SPRING ARTWORK

In 1573, the painter Giuseppe Arcimboldo presented a series of four composite portraits representing the four seasons. The woman in *Spring* is made up entirely of vegetation, particularly flowers. How many species do you recognize?

Among the numerous plant species are peonies, roses, wild roses, anemones, lilies and even a cabbage!

DELBŒUF ILLUSIONS

Compare the size of the two center circles.
Which is bigger?

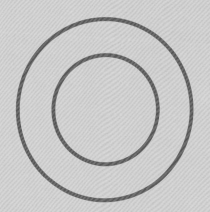

The two circles are identical. However, the one on the right appears bigger because it is placed at the center of a circle with only a slightly larger diameter. The circle on the left is surrounded by a circle that is much bigger, which leads us to overestimate the size of the circle in its center. The Belgium psychologist Delbœuf analyzed this effect in the 19th century.

EXTRAPOLATED CUBE

Which figure do you
reconstitute when
you look at these
eight circles?

A cube seems to appear
even though there isn't
a cube in this image.
Guided by the marks
in the white disks, we
reconstitute the shape of
a cube because, guided
by our memory, we
organize the void to make
sense of it.

COUNT THE CIRCLES

How many circles do you think there are in this image?

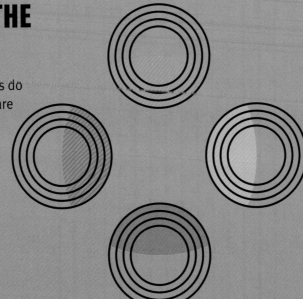

Only 16! The colored areas that pass under the circles create the illusion of a big circle. The illusion is so strong that we have the impression of seeing a dark disk appear.

A MAN AND A WOMAN

What did you see first, a man playing the saxophone or the face of a woman?

The quasi-absence of details makes your brain work overtime to associate the black shape with a known figure. If you look at the left side of the drawing, you see a saxophonist in profile, with the mouthpiece of the instrument becoming the woman's nose when you look to the right. It's pictorial ambiguity!

A QUESTION OF HEMISPHERES

Can you manage to say, aloud, the color of the words before reading the words themselves?

YELLOW BLUE RED
ORANGE BLACK GREEN
BLUE YELLOW RED
GREEN BLACK ORANGE
RED BLUE YELLOW
ORANGE BLACK GREEN

It's hard not to stumble since the two hemispheres of your brain are in conflict: the right side perceives color, while the left recognizes the word (which it does faster than the right recognizes the color). Hence there's interference when you read aloud.

THE SHAPE OF EMPTINESS

What shape does this group of lines form?

We mentally reconstruct disks that don't actually exist. It's a subjective illusion: we unconsciously look for a familiar shape in the scattered arrangement of small lines.

BIG BROTHER IS WATCHING YOU

What happens when you do a quick sweep of this image?

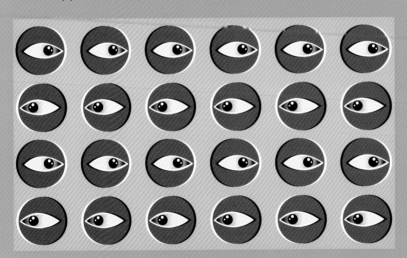

We have trouble focusing our gaze because we are alternating from left to right, following the direction of the pupils in the drawing. Hence, we have the impression that the eyes are moving and that some are spying on us.

FLAWED VIEW

What are you able to read on this image? If nothing comes to you, squint your eyes or move the image back and try again.

The text says that you have "bad eyes."

COTTAGE

Is this image a photomontage?

No. The photo has not been retouched, yet the cottage looks like a computer drawing. In reality, it is painted directly on the wall of the white building.

HELP! THIEF!

Can you help the peasant woman find the bandits hiding in the landscape?

They're in the tree, on the left. Turn the drawing upside down and you'll see three profiles hiding in the grooves of the trunk, two facing each other near the base of the trunk and another at the base of the branches.

THE FRASER SPIRAL

Does this spiral draw your eyes in?

It does, but it's not a spiral — it's a series of concentric circles! The combination of a regular pattern (the circles) and a contrasting pattern (the colored bands) along with the succession of tilted elements encourage the perception of imaginary twists and turns. This illusion was named after the psychologist James Fraser.

AN INFLATED FIGURE

Are the angles of this quadrilateral shape straight?

Even though the drawing represents a perfect square, the circles drive the brain to curve the sides. You can check if it truly is a square by measuring the angles with the help of a protractor.

NUANCE

Are these four semicircles the same shade of gray?

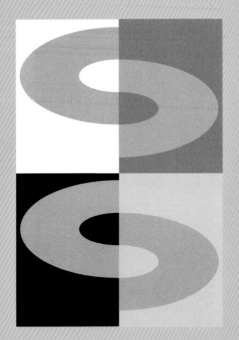

Yes, but the four different background colors alter our perception of the shades of gray: on a light background, the semicircle appears darker, and on a black or dark gray background it's the opposite.

THE PENROSE TRIANGLE

Would you be able to
reproduce this three-
chevron construction?

This object is spatially
absurd. The three beams with
overlapping parallel lines
are drawn using different
perspectives. Each beam is
perpendicular to the other
two. British mathematician
and physicist Roger Penrose
published this drawing in 1958
in a journal of psychology.

AN INSPIRED PORTRAIT

Who is hiding in the features of this mustachioed man?

Up close, you can see that five women make up the drawing. There are three on the forehead, of which the body of one extends to form the left cheek and the arm of another makes up the nose, and there is also a torso for the right eye and a final woman forming the man's chin.

STRETCHABLE CIRCLES

Are the four circles around the middle ring perfectly circular?

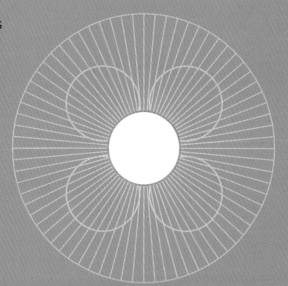

Yes they are, but the radiating lines in the background disrupt our perception. These lines give the impression that the circles are stretched out lengthwise, toward the exterior of the figure.

A BLUE RECTANGLE

Stare at the black dot for a few seconds. What happens?

The green rectangles disappear! This illusion is linked to the Troxler effect, named after the Swiss scientist who described the phenomenon in 1804. We lose our peripheral vision when we stare intensely in front of us.

MOVING RINGS

Stare at these rings for a few seconds. In which direction do you see them turn?

The impression of movement is created by the patterns on the rings. They seem to turn in the direction of the rounded half moons. Hence, the small circle on the bottom right seems to turn clockwise, contrary to the big circle in the middle.

ARCS

Which of the three arcs is the most curved?

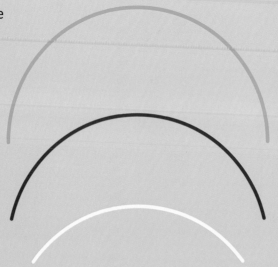

The three lines seem to be curved at different angles, but they are all identical. Only the lengths of the arcs vary, making the short arcs seem flatter than the longer arcs — hence the illusion that the yellow and pink arcs are less curved than the blue one!

VERSATILE COLORS

Do the horizontal lines seem darker in the rectangle on the
left or the one on the right?

They are the same shade
of pink! However, the pale
background gives the
impression that the lines
on the right are darker.
It's called the Bezold
effect: our perception of
hues is modified by an
increase in the intensity
of light.

A VERY UNORTHODOX SQUARE

Does this figure have any right angles?

Yes it does; it's a perfect square. If it seems deformed, it's because the hatching pattern in the background appears to "stretch" the angles of the square. The psychologist William Orbison described this optical illusion in 1939.

LINES AND CUBES

Are these squares equidistant?

Yes, they all are, but the presence of the white arrows interferes with our perception of the information and our ability to compare the distances. When the arrows are facing each other, they seem to shrink the space between the squares.

BETWEEN TWO AGES

This drawing, entitled *My Wife and My Mother-in-Law*, was published in 1915. Do you see both women?

In this drawing by cartoonist H.E. Hill, we can see two profiles: a young woman with her head turned away and an old woman with her eyes cast down. The necklace of the young woman serves as the mouth of the older one.

PUZZLE STAIRCASE

Is this staircase going up or down?

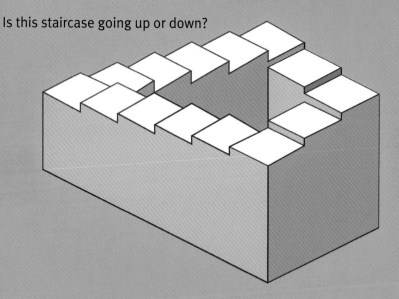

You can go up or down this staircase perpetually! Each element of the structure can work as a stair, but the connections are such that the figure as a whole is incoherent: the staircase has three right angles that lead back to the starting point.

CONCAVE OR CONVEX?

What does this image represent: a flat surface or an elevated one?

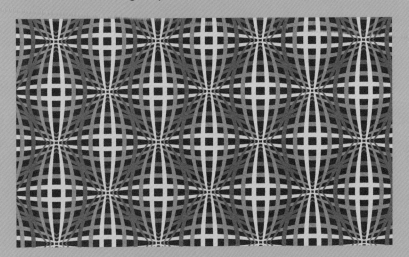

It is a flat surface, but the repetition of the pattern and the perspective it creates make the image look embossed. The optical illusion is not the result of defective eyesight: it's your brain misleading you!

GEOMETRIC AMBIGUITY

Are these figures sunken or in relief?

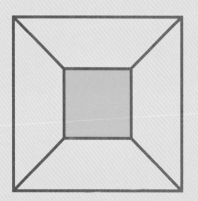

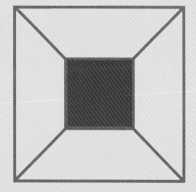

Although they are executed in two dimensions, these drawings give the impression being three-dimensional objects. The colored squares simultaneously create the illusion of depth and height. We imagine at once a pyramid viewed from above and a wall at the back of a room.

MOUNTING KIT

Would you take the risk of building this shelf?

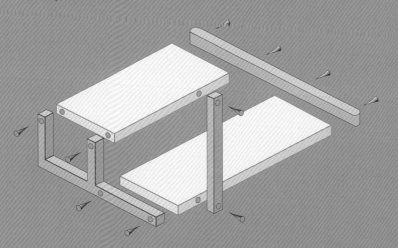

You'd end up with a very unstructured piece of furniture! It's impossible to join the pieces, although the orientation of the perspective is correct. The vertical bar can't be attached to both shelves at the same time since they're not on the same plane; the same applies to the side bar on the right.

MOSAIC

Which of the two black squares is bigger?

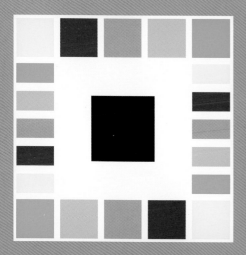

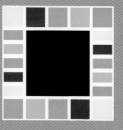

Neither is bigger. They are identical. The proximity of the colored pattern in the background confuses our ability to estimate the dimensions. We always analyze patterns in relation to their environment.

TWO DOTS, TWO MEASUREMENTS

Which of the two squares is bigger?

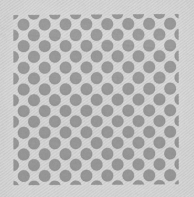

They are identical, but the size and number of blue dots create the illusion that the square on the right is bigger than the one on the left.

CIRCULAR

What shapes
do you see?

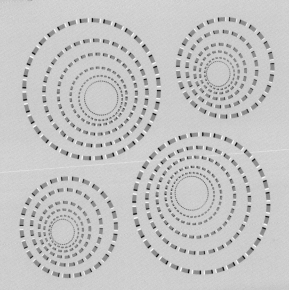

You no doubt get the
impression of seeing spirals,
but they are actually circles.
This illusion is due to the fact
that the little rectangles that
make up the circles are off
center and are alternating
black and white stripes.

FLOATING POULTRY?

What suggests that this roast chicken has not yet been placed on the table?

The "patch" in the foreground creates the illusion of being a shadow cast by the plate as it hovers over the table. We use such graphic elements to help us situate objects in their space.

A CONVOLUTED ARCHWAY

In which way is this design completely irrational?

This figure is impossible because its spatial characteristics contradict each other. The position of the archways on the checkerboard does not respect the rules of perspective, which creates the illusion of multiple surfaces.

THE ILLUSION OF THE SQUARE

Which shape do you see when you look at this rectangle from a distance?

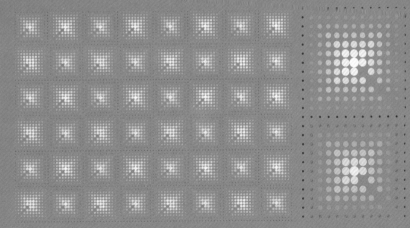

An orange and a purple checkerboard appear on the left. On the right, the two shapes are close-ups of each of the colored squares that make up the checkerboard. These are not actually squares. They are an illusion created by the layout of the colored dots of varying sizes.

CIRCULATION

Which of these three vans is the biggest?

The vans in this photomontage are all the same size. However, we perceive the vehicle at the front of the line to be the biggest since it takes up more space on the street! We understand objects in space by looking at them in perspective: the furthest away is usually seen as the smallest, but we take the environment into consideration.

A BAG OF KNOTS

Would you be able
to undo this knot?

It's impossible! In fact, if you
trace the rope with a pencil,
you'll never arrive at the end.
The outlines of the drawing
are ambiguous, making us
question whether we're seeing
part of the object or not. The
effect is reinforced by the lack
of braiding lines on part of
the rope.

FOUR PHANTOM LINES

What letter do you see when you look at this square?

It's an X. The overlaying of numerous squares — from smaller to smaller and from lighter to lighter — creates two white rays. These lines don't, however, actually exist. This optical phenomenon is called the Vasarely illusion and is named after a painter who developed a science of colors in his work.

FURRY LINES

Are the orange lines parallel?

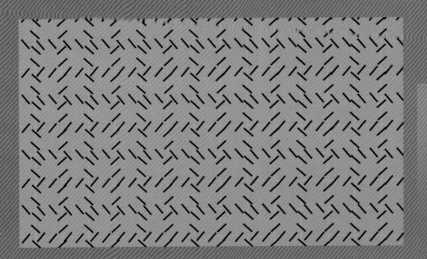

Yes, but the short black lines disrupt our perception. Our brain seeks to transform the sharp angles created by the short black lines and orange lines into right angles, thereby "slanting" the lines toward each another. German astrophysicist Zöllner outlined this illusion in the 19th century.

FLAT OR THREE-DIMENSIONAL?

Which detail proves that this juxtaposition of cubes is impossible?

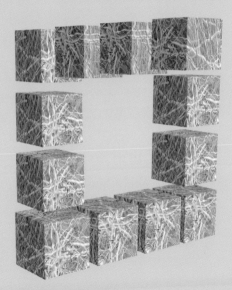

The row of cubes on the top is not arranged according to the same perspective as the others. The spatial information is incorrect for a 3-D structure.

APPARITION

Stare at the bird's eye for 20 seconds and then at the cage.
What happens?

The silhouette of the bird appears in purple! It's a retinal illusion: the white of the cage contrasts with the yellow of the bird illustration, creating a purple light since purple is yellow's complementary color.

A DECEPTIVE SUN

Is this woman a magician?

Photography, being a 2-D visual medium, flattens elevations. Therefore, a photo cancels out perspective, modifying the scale of objects. In this photo, the woman in the foreground seems to be holding the setting sun in the palm of her hand, but the sun is actually in the background.

HABITUS LINGUISTICUS

How many Fs are in this text?

FINISHED FILES ARE THE RESULT OF YEARS OF
SCIENTIFIC STUDY COMBINED WITH THE
EXPERIENCE OF YEARS

Did you count three Fs? Most people do. There are, in fact, six! The word "of" is so familiar to us that we tend to simply skip over it, without counting its F.

IDENTICAL RINGS?

Are these two circles identical?

They are the same, but the pyramid modifies our perception, making the top circle appear as though it's not perfectly round.

A LIVE FACADE

Where does the trompe l'oeil begin on these buildings?

All of the facades to the left of the building with the closed white shutters (in the middle of the photo) are in fact painted illusions!

A DISCREET FELINE

Where is the tiger?

The tiger is hiding in the background, behind the huts. He is stretched out in profile, his back creating the mountain range beneath the sun.

LIGHT AND DARK

Is the background color of this rectangle uniform?

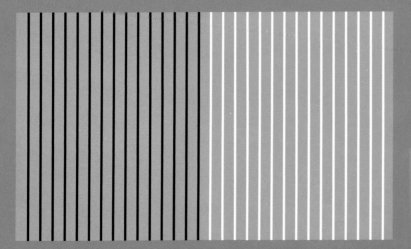

Yes. The section with black stripes appears darker than the one with white stripes because the color of the stripes influences how we perceive the background color.

BARBED WIRE

Are these four lines parallel?

Yes they are, but the fact that they are two-toned and bordered with a pattern confuses our perception, giving us the impression that they are slanted.

MOVE YOUR HEAD

What happens when you stare at the center of this image?

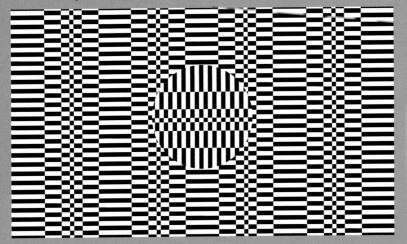

The circle seems to levitate above the background and even move from side to side. This illusion is created by using the same pattern on the background and on the circle but rotating it 90 degrees on the circle.

LITTLE YELLOW DOTS

Stare at one of the yellow dots for a few seconds.
What happens?

The other dots disappear! This illusion is due to our peripheral vision being disrupted when we stare at one spot, which "smooths out" the rest of the environment.

THE BIGGER OF THE TWO

Which do you think is the bigger of the two squares?

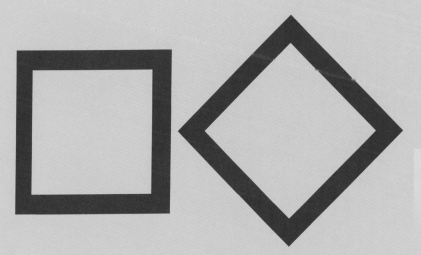

They are identical. But since one of the squares is positioned on a point, its sides are not parallel to the page, which makes it difficult to compare the two figures.

CUT LINE

Are the two slanted lines in this image aligned?

Yes they are, but since they each intersect a parallel line, it gives the impression that they are offset. The slanted lines actually form the ends of a virtual straight line. This illusion is called the Poggendorff illusion and is named after a 19th-century German physicist.

COGS AND GEARS

What happens when you look at these gears?

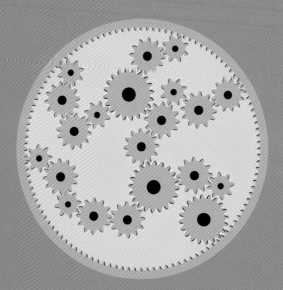

They start turning! When the eye sends an image to the brain, the brain interprets the message according to a known construction. The brain always tries to make sense of things, so it will create movement that is known to it.

REAL OR FAKE CHECKERBOARD?

What do you see when you look at this yellow and purple checkerboard?

The small yellow and purple squares create a virtual circle on the retina, disturbing our perception of the lines that make up the board. The lines appear to be curved and in relief, when they are in fact straight.

PERCHED BIRDS

Are these three branches the same length?

Yes they are, even though the bottom one seems shorter. It's the position of the birds and, especially, the position of the horizontal branches that mislead us. The more off center the intersection of the horizontal line with the vertical line, the longer the horizontal line looks.

APPARITIONS

What happens when you move this image sideways while staring at the black dot in the middle?

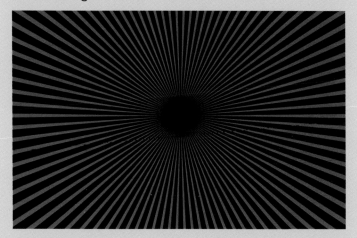

Rosettelike shapes erupt and swirl around the black dot in the center. This illusion is caused by the color gradation of the rays.

THE RING

What do you see when you stare at the figure in the center of this image for a few seconds?

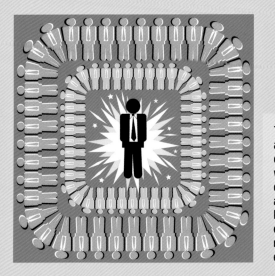

The little men start to move around him! The illusion is created by our peripheral vision: the layout and repeated colors of the figures produces an imaginary movement. Moreover, the white and black outlines alternate in both rings, creating shadows and elevations.

WATCH THE UV!

Stare at the white disk for a few seconds.
What appears around it?

The zigzags formed by the rays around the white dot create concentric circles. The strong contrast with the blue background reinforces the illusion of light being diffused.

THE TOWER

Is this construction possible in reality?

No it's not, since the tower, clearly visible with height at the top, transforms itself into a hallowed and confusing structure at the base of the building.

CAMOUFLAGE

Look at this portrait then stare at a white surface. Whom do you recognize?

Like in a photo negative after processing, Che Guevara appears as a residual image!

TRANSFORMATION

Do these two photos show the same building?

Yes. It's simply a trompe l'oeil that's been painted on the facade and a signpost that's been added in the garden.

EINSTEIN?

Look at this portrait up close and then from far away. What do you notice?

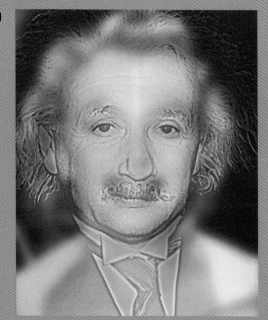

Close up we see Albert Einstein, and from far away Marilyn Monroe appears! The distance alters our perception of the variations of contrast, leaving our brain to sort through them.

HYPNOSIS

What happens when you stare at this image?

The circles start moving and even seem to move closer to us. This image sends way too much information at once to our brain to allow us to focus, which disturbs our perception.

UNDER THE LIGHTS

Scan this image with your eyes. What happens?

The purple circles seem to be sending out light! This vibration effect happens when your eye jumps from one image to the next. You subconsciously remember the white dot and superimpose it onto the next dot. The black patterns dissipate your gaze, and the contrast between the light and dark areas intensify the brightness.

A COLOR PUZZLE

Look at the middle square on the top surface of the cube: it's brown. Now look at the middle square on the surface at the front. What color is it?

Lighter? Well no, actually, it's not! It's the same color. It's the shadow projected onto the front surface of the cube that creates this illusion. In fact, it creates a dark area around the middle square, and surrounded by darker squares, the middle square looks lighter than the top surface, which is exposed to full light.

RIGHT ANGLES

Do you recognize the blue shapes?

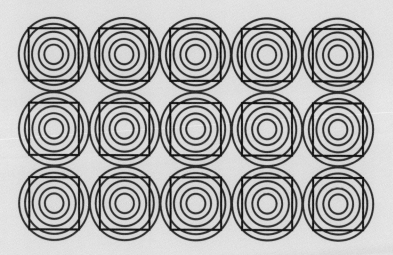

They are squares! However, the presence of the pink concentric circles in the background distorts our perception of the shapes: their sides appear to be curving toward the center.

FREE FALL

Is this parachute realistic?

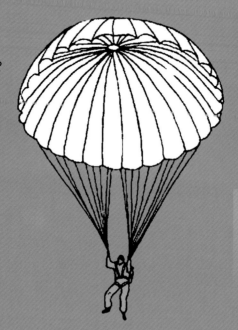

No. It's the drawing of an impossible parachute. At first glance, we think we see the canopy from underneath, but the lines distort our perception, and when we stare at them, we have the impression of seeing the parachute from above.

THE HIDDEN CIRCLE

What do you see
when you stare
at this drawing?

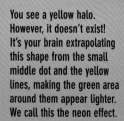

You see a yellow halo.
However, it doesn't exist!
It's your brain extrapolating
this shape from the small
middle dot and the yellow
lines, making the green area
around them appear lighter.
We call this the neon effect.

DON QUIXOTE

What do you see in this 1989 painting by Mexican artist Octavio Ocampo?

You see Don Quixote! However, if you look more closely, you'll see the blades of the windmills against which he battled (the hair) and this same Don Quixote on horseback (the neck and left eye) accompanied by his loyal horseman Sancho Panza (the right eye). A number of faces and animal heads surround them.

TARGET THE COLOR

Are the gray portions
of the numbered circles
the same shade?

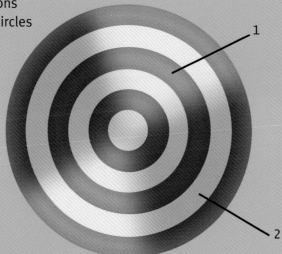

Yes. Zone 1 seems
darker than zone 2.
This illusion is created
by the variations of
light and shadow that
cross the drawing.

ROLLING AND SWAYING

The water level is not parallel with the top of the table.
How is this possible?

The three glasses were glued to a board that was then tilted. The photo has been altered to position the table horizontally, masking the trickery.

PREPOSTEROUS

Do you think this figure
can exist in reality?

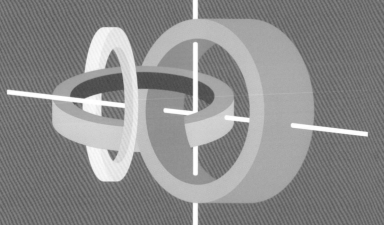

If you look at this image
carefully, you'll quickly notice
that the twists the three
interwoven rings make are
impossible. We'd have to
reverse the positions of the
parts of the drawing that are
hidden for the figure to respect
the rules of perspective.

GRAY DIAMONDS

Are all the lines of diamonds the same shade of white?

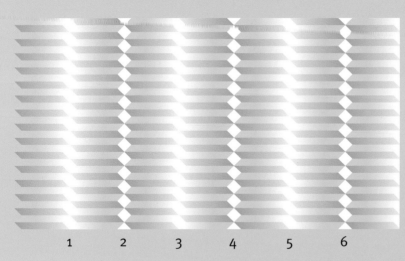

Lines 1, 3 and 5 seem, mistakenly, to be darker. This impression is simply due to the fact that the background is lighter under these lines than it is under the three other lines. The eye integrates these variations of brightness when it perceives the diamonds' shade of white.

WHERE IS THE MIDDLE?

Is the middle of this circle the pink dot or the blue dot?

The yellow arcs distort our sense of the distance in this image as well as our perception of the center, which is, in fact, the pink dot.

WEIRD WALLPAPER

Stare at this image. Does it appear to be 2-D or 3-D?

It appears 3-D. The succession of graphic elements becoming more and more inclined produces a flaring out of the lines from left to right, creating the illusion of a curved surface. The eye is led to perceive turns where there aren't any.

HIGH VOLTAGE

Does everything in this image look realistic to you?

At first glance yes, but the metal structure on the lower right side renders the drawing's spatial orientation ambiguous. We don't know if we're seeing the scene from the top or the bottom. By turning the image over, the dancer appears to be suspended.

WATCH YOUR STEP!

Is this really an imminent catastrophe?

No, it is obviously an illusion. The photographer positioned himself at ground level, near the feet of the person in the foreground, and has played around with the perspective to make the vehicle in the background appear as though it's being threatened by a giant's foot.

JAWS

Does this fisherman have any hope of escaping from this great white shark?

Lucky for him, the animal is actually much less imposing! This shot is not, however, a photomontage. Its huge depth of field renders the foreground and background equally focused. In addition, the lighting reinforces the disproportion between the subjects, which creates the illusion that the shark is threatening the man.

BULL'S-EYE

What shape are the two figures in the middle of this image?

They are squares, but the numerous concentric circles mislead your brain, making it look like the sides of the figures are curved. You can check the straightness of the angles for yourself with the help of a ruler or protractor.

DOUBLE VISION

What do you see
in this colored
shape?

This figure suggests two
visual interpretations,
either the core of an
apple or two profiles
facing each other.

DIAGONAL READING

Are these letters tilted?

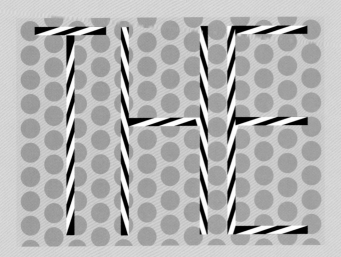

The vertical lines of these three letters are, in fact, parallel. However, the angled pattern that covers them makes us believe they are leaning.

A BOX OF BARS

Is this assembly
of shapes
logical?

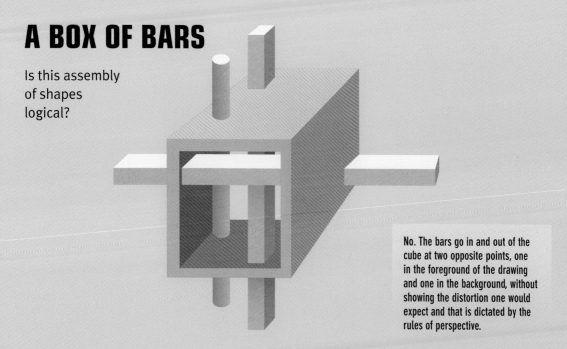

No. The bars go in and out of the
cube at two opposite points, one
in the foreground of the drawing
and one in the background, without
showing the distortion one would
expect and that is dictated by the
rules of perspective.

A NARROW WAIST?

Which of these two figures is bigger?

These two series of lines form two identical squares, but the square on the right appears bigger. This is because horizontal lines have a tendency to swell a shape, whereas vertical lines elongate. A useful trick when choosing your clothes!

ONE CIRCLE CAN HIDE ANOTHER

Is the small circle on the right perfectly round?

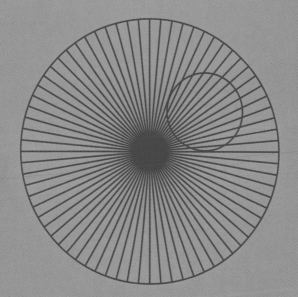

Yes! The rays and the blurred disk in the center distort the small circle and make it seem oval. We have trouble focusing because we're receiving contradictory information.

LET YOURSELF BE ENCHANTED

Stare the center of the image. What do you see?

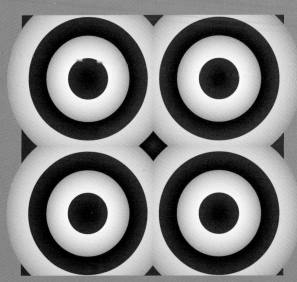

The neon yellow rings seem to pull away from and even animate the purple circles! These two colors are complementary, so their juxtaposition produces a strong contrast. This effect is intensified by the color gradation between the circles, which gives the impression that the image is "breathing."

SEALED FRAMES

Is it possible to construct an assembly of frames such as this one?

No. This construction is impossible because the angles spatially contradict each other. The faces of the frames transform themselves into internal walls.

DFIFIUCLT TO RAED?

Can you read this text?

Can you read this? Accdoring to a Unirvesity of Cambirdge stduy, the odrer of the lettres in a word aren't imtporant. The olny thnig that marttes is that the fisrt and lsat letrtes be in the rihgt palce. The rset of the ltteers can be comletpely disrderoed, and you can still raed whitout any prolembs. That's beucase we do not read leettr by letter but ecah wrod as wolhe.

Just as when we are trying to decipher a foreign language, we lean on the context and our lexical knowledge and experience to form words that make sense.

A JUMBLE OF VEGETABLES

What is this bowl of vegetables hiding?

Turn the page upside down and you'll see the portrait of *The Vegetable Gardener*, which was painted in 1590 by Arcimboldo.

ARCHITECTURE OF DREAMS

Does this architecture seem logical to you?

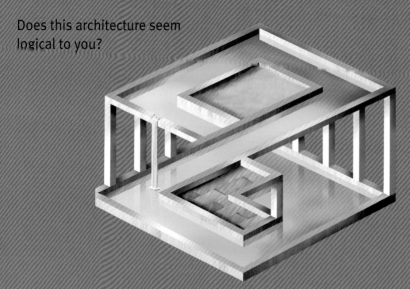

It shouldn't! The roof and the ground floor of this strange building seem to meet, creating a perpetual figure eight that is totally impossible in the real world.

A STRONG BOTTLE OF WATER

Is this a photomontage or is the man really balancing himself on a bottle of water?

In reality, the man is positioned much farther away from the photographer than the bottle is. The shot blurs the notion of distance between the foreground and background, making the person and the bottle appear to be in the same spot. The incline of the horizon intensifies the illusion.

ILLUSION-OPTER

Which is the longer line, the red or the purple?

It's the purple one! We perceive the red line as being longer since it's within a circle, and we interpret the red line as being the circle's diameter. Since the blue surface is bigger than the pink one, we infer that the red line must be longer. The illusion comes from the fact that these are ellipses, not circles.

SURFING THE WEB

Move your gaze around the web. What do you see?

Blue dots seem to be blinking where the lines intersect! This is the effect of retinal persistence. When we stare at a bright white dot, the image is imprinted on the eye's retina, but in reverse. As soon as we stare at another white dot, the residual image superimposes itself onto that dot. When you move your eyes around the image, that rapid movement produces a blinking effect.

WHERE IS TOM THUMB?

Despite his long legs, this ogre doesn't manage to catch Tom Thumb. Do you see where he is hidden?

He's not very far, but he is well hidden! Only his face is visible, concealed in profile between the arm, the sword and the torso of the ogre.

FROM THE OTHER SIDE OF THE MIRROR

From where was this photo taken?

We have the impression of being on top of the landscape and seeing into another world, but in reality it's only a puddle of water. The reflection of the sky and the trees in the water creates a very striking effect!

AN UNREAL OBJECT

Do you think this object could be reproduced in three dimensions?

This object can only exist as a drawing. It's a 2-D image, but your eyes interpret it as a 3-D object. Paradoxically, your brain ascertains that the spatial indicators are contradictory and that the object is completely impossible in 3-D!

IN THREE DIMENSIONS

What effect do
these four figures
produce?

These four warped squares
have a stacked symmetrical
pattern. This game of curves,
which gets smaller and
smaller, produces a surface
effect that is both concave
and convex at the same time.
The center of the drawing
thereby looks domed, while
the centers of the four figure
appear hollow.

HIDE AND SEEK

What is concealed within the spots in this drawing?

Look closely at the center: a dalmatian appears, sniffing the ground with his snout.

LINES AND TILES

Are the vertical lines in this image parallel?

They are, but the color gradation being reversed from one column to the next makes them appear slanted.

ARROW STAIRS

How many
arrows can you
count in this
image?

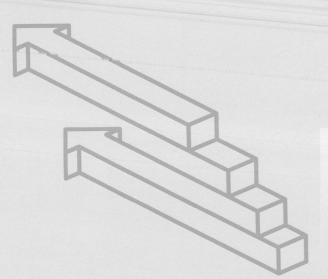

Only the arrow on top is
fully formed! Your eyes
perceive many different
three-dimensional forms
within these objects, but
they mutually exclude each
other even though they are
all presented together. We
therefore cannot clearly
interpret this image.

MIRROR EFFECT

How many buildings do you see in this photo?

There are three. Contrary to what you might believe, the mirrored surface of the building is not reflecting the building on the right but rather a building not shown in the photo. The similar colors create the illusion.

TRAP THE BUBBLE

Are the red dots aligned?

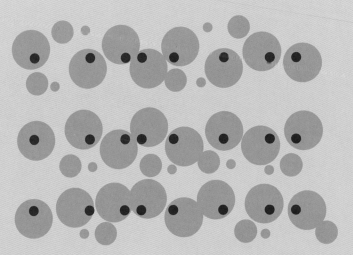

You can, in fact, link the three series of red dots and thus form three parallel lines! It is the orange circles that confuse our interpretation of the linearity of this image.

DECOR

What pattern is adorning the curtains in the foreground of this photo?

They are squares. Contrary to what you may believe, the wavy lines are not a pattern. They are rays of light that are filtered by shutters and distorted by the pleated curtain.

273

GET TO THE POINT

Do you see straight lines or a moving pattern?

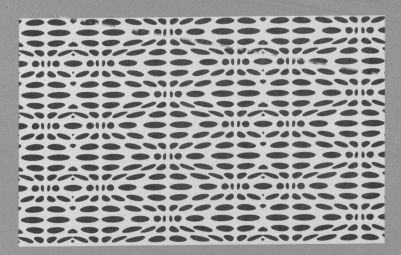

Your perception of this image fluctuates depending on whether you focus your eyes on the curves or the horizontal lines.

IMAGINARY REVOLUTION

Does looking at these disks make you feel dizzy?

Yes, since your eyes tire when you stare at an object. In addition, the direction of the patterns is reversed on each disk from top to bottom and from left to right. The illusion of rotation erupts at the moment when the images you were staring at, now fixed in your memory, enter in conflict with the ones that are shifting from the movement of your eyes.

CONTRASTING WALLPAPER

Do you see foliage or a pattern in relief?

Depending on whether you focus your eyes on the color yellow or the color orange, the series of patterns stand out in the foreground or in the background.

A BLACK HOLE

What do the graphic elements in this image remind you of?

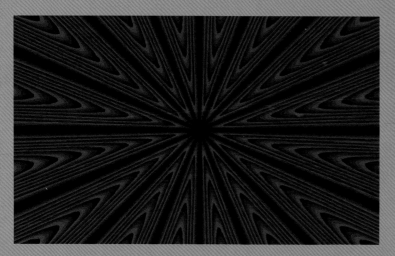

We get an impression of depth because the curved red patterns converge toward the black center of the figure, attracting the gaze toward the vanishing point of this image.

A LOST LILLIPUTIAN?

Is this tiny being an elf or maybe a leprechaun?

It's just a man. Due to its large depth of field, this photo plays with perspective. We get the impression that the subject is in the foreground, in the palm of someone's hand, but he's really sitting much farther away, in the background.

LIGHT AND PERSPECTIVE

What does this image represent?

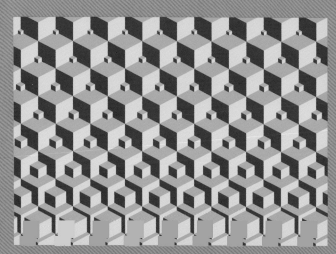

When we perceive the light as coming from the right, a series of cubes seems to pile up, between which are placed smaller and smaller cubes. If we perceive the cubes as being lit from the left, then we see an elevated mosaic that is made up of hexagons with concave centers.

PARALLEL WORLDS

Are the red
lines curved?

It's the Wundt illusion.
The vertical red lines are
straight and parallel, but
they can appear curved.
The green lines in the
background produce the
distortion.

BETWEEN EARTH AND SKY

What is this patch of grass doing in the sky?

This photo is actually showing a puddle of water that is reflecting the sky.

AT NIGHT, ALL DOTS ARE GRAY

How many shades of gray do you see in the dots of this image?

The series of dots are the same color, but the variation of the white and gray backgrounds modifies our perception.

HIDDEN HUNTERS

How many hunters are waiting to ambush the antelopes?

We can see four faces in profile: two are upside down, hiding on each side of the entrance to the cave on the right; another profile is visible behind the antelope in the foreground, behind its tail, on the ground and facing up; and the last one is on the left side of the image and looks like a rock.

DEATH BECOMES YOU

Move up close to the image then move away from it. What do you see?

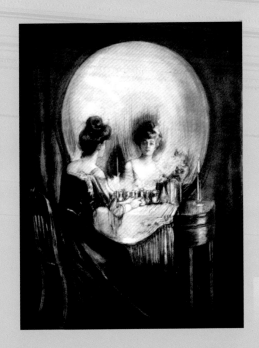

There are two images in one: a woman admiring herself in a mirror and a skull.

BE SQUARE

How many hidden squares can you count in this image?

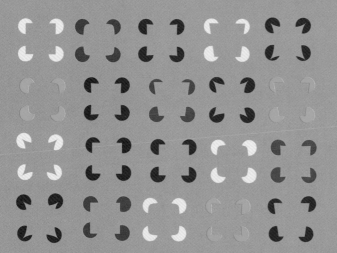

There are four squares (the first figure in the first line, the second and third figures in the third line and the fourth figure in the fourth line). The other 16 figures are also quadrilateral shapes, but they have either obtuse or sharp angles or are rectangles. It's the phenomenon of subjective contours: the brain reconstitutes shapes that don't exist.

BACKGROUND AND SHAPE

Is this polygon actually a square?

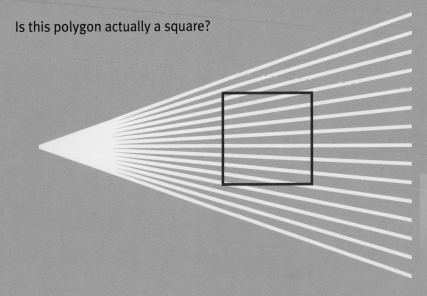

Yes it is, but the lines in the background create a perspective that visually distorts the angles. If you look at the square, it seems to float in the lines and its sides look uneven.

A FIELD OF PRIMROSES

Scan this image with your eyes. What happens?

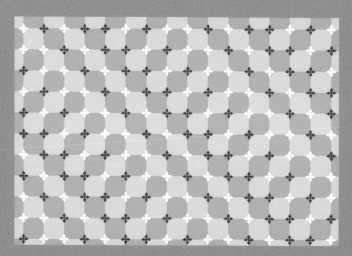

The surface undulates!
This impressive illusion of movement is created by the alternating light and dark colors and the shapes of the patterns. The strong contrast alters our perception of the checkerboard. The white and pink "flowers" round out the angles of the green squares and cause our gaze to "slide" diagonally.

SACRED PERSPECTIVE

Which effect creates the perspective in Antonio del Pollaiuolo's *Annunciation* (1470)?

The painter created perspective around a vanishing point that is not centered but rather left of center. This choice spotlights the angel, the messenger of God who announced to Mary that she was pregnant with a divine child.

RETIREMENT

Are you able to read this text?

AND HOERE, RES!OLVING TO HAR^ASS MYFSELF NO MO,RE,
I AM PREPGARING FOR A LOVNGER JOU*RNEY THAN ALL
THSESE, HANVING LIVE)D 72 YEOARS A LI'FE OF INFKINITE
VACRIETY AND HAVRING LEARINED SUFFICRIENTLY TO KNIOW
THE VAFLUE OF RETIHREMENT AND THE BLEJSSING OF
ENDAING OUR DARYS IN PEADCE.

EXCERPT FROM *ROBINSON CRUSOE* BY DANIEL DEFOE

It's easier than it seems
at first! We are, in a way,
conditioned by our learning
and our practice of reading.
Instinctively, we identify the
correct words despite the extra
letters and symbols.

WHERE IS THE HORSE?

This cavalryman is ready to leave on a long trip, but his ride has disappeared. Can you find it?

The horse's head is drawn in the cavalryman's shirtfront.

COLOR APPRECIATION

Which green column is darker?

At first glance, the column on the right looks darker, but they are actually the same shade of green. We perceive the color differently depending on whether the blue bands overlap the columns or cross underneath them.

ZIGZAGS

Do you see a spiral?

You certainly do, but it's fake! The zigzag patterns create the illusion. The direction of the notches and the alternation of the color orange on the bands with the transparent background make us perceive a circle at each level.

HEAD SHOT

Is this a photomontage?

No it's not. It's a classic vacationers' game: a boy is buried up to his head in the sand, and a woman is lying just behind him and concealing her head in a ditch.

TARGET

Stare at the black dot for a few seconds and then look at the white rectangle. What do you see?

If a pink heart with a blue outline appears, it's normal. Retinal persistence causes the complementary colors for green (red) and yellow (purple) to appear, but they are dimmed by a partial restitution due to ocular fatigue, which creates pink and blue.

ANGLES

Stare at the quadrilaterals in this image. Are they square?

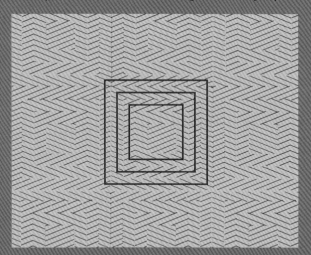

Yes. The variation of the background patterns creates visual confusion. The orientation of the background lines distorts our perception of the right angles of the three squares.

BETWEEN EARTH AND SKY

Has this photo been retouched?

No it hasn't, but grass isn't growing in the sky! It's a photo of the reflection of a building in a puddle of water.

FAKE CUTS

Are these red
lines continuous?

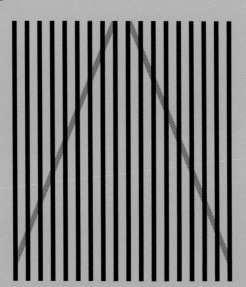

Yes. We have trouble perceiving
the continuity of the two red
lines because the parallel black
lines intersect them at regular
intervals, giving the illusion of a
dotted line.

VERTICAL ILLUSION

Are the vertical lines parallel or slanted?

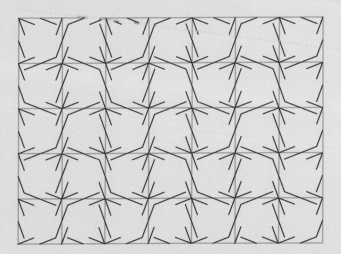

They seem to meet, but they are actually parallel. The red patterns prevent our eyes from focusing, and their orientation leads our eyes in a particular direction, creating the illusion of slanted lines.

ARITHMETIC

How many blocks are in
this structure?

It's impossible to determine!
This drawing is composed
of open and closed shapes.
To the left and right of the
image, we see the extremities
of three beams, or six in total.
But if we count up the middle
of the structure, only the ends
of four blocks are visible!

WATCH FOR THE SPOTS

Look at the small white square under the second row from the top. What do you see?

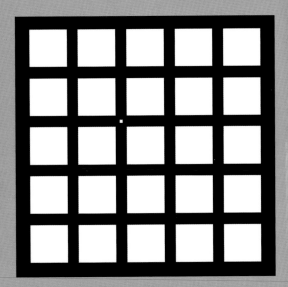

Gray dots seem to be dancing where the black lines intersect, except where the small white square is located. Through retinal persistence, this dot prevents the strong contrast between the white squares and the black lines from creating the gray dot.

A QUIRKY STRUCTURE

In what way is this figure
unrealistic?

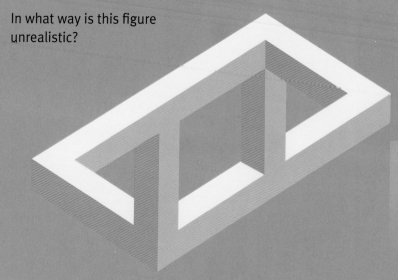

This structure is impossible.
The two bars that are shown in
perspective and on the same
plane seem to be supporting
the left side of the frame, as
if that section is on a different
level. These are paradoxical
joints, however, since the
surface of the frame is flat.

SLIDING BRICKS

What happens when you quickly look at the image from top to bottom?

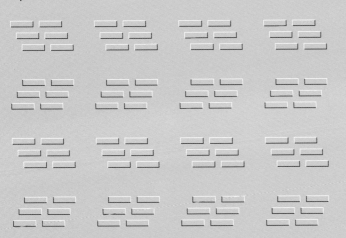

The small bricks seem to be moving from left to right. This visual confusion is created by the drawings of the shadows being cast by the bricks, which alternate from being directed toward the bottom to toward the top.

AN IMPOSSIBLE OBJECT

Would you know
how to create this
object at home?

You would be wasting your
time! This representation
is part of the category of
objects known as "impossible"
and defies the laws of
geometry. Swedish artist Oscar
Reutersvärd was one of the
first to create these figures; he
conceived more than 2,500!

AMBIGUITY

What do you see in the foreground of this image?

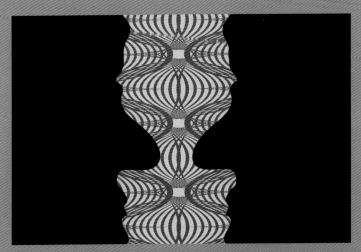

Depending on whether you're looking at the colored shape or the black sections of the image, you see a vase or two symmetrical human profiles.

MIRAGE IN THE DESERT

Where do the palm trees end and the camels begin?

It's difficult to determine since the gradation between the foreground and the background produces a fading effect.

IMAGINARY SHAPES

Do you only see diamonds among these patterns?

The white diamonds are clearly identifiable, but if you stare at the background color at the corners of the image, you'll see purple arrows appear, pointing in the direction of each corner of the square.

A MIRACULOUS APPARITION

Stare at the image for 30 seconds and then move your gaze to a white surface. Who do you see?

The figure of Jesus! It's a residual image. The illusion is not created in the brain but in the retina: orange, being brighter than black, impresses itself on the retina and is restored on the white surface.

PROFILES

How many figures appear here?

We see the profile of a blonde woman wearing a fur collar, but by turning the image upside down, a Russian woman wearing a fur hat appears.

A ROAD TO NOWHERE

Where did the figure on the right come from?

He came from nowhere! The road transforms itself into a wall. The artist created a paradoxical game of perspective that breaks the continuity of surfaces and elevations.

THE FISHBOWL

Stare at the fish in the bowl for 30 seconds and then move your gaze to the fishbowl. What happens?

The fish seems to appear in the bowl, under the nose of the cat! This illusion is what we call a "residual" image, which is an image that persists on the retina even after your eyes have moved to a new object.

SCARY DANCE

What do you see within these linear patterns?

Squint and you'll see a skull appear in the middle of the image! Even though its contours are not outlined, we can make out the shape of a skull due to the contrasting vertical and horizontal lines.

THE LAUGHING MAN

With whom is this old man laughing?

If you turn the image upside down, you'll see a second laughing man with a bandana on his head. This image, produced by Épinal, is among the artist's many riddles, which often involved upside-down figures.

TWINS

Are these two children perfectly identical?

No! Not all of the boy on the right is upside down — his eyes and mouth are in the same direction as his twin on the left. The brain handles vertical symmetry very badly; we interpret an upside-down image globally, without noticing the details. Turn the photo around, and the difference between the two boys becomes clearer.

A PYRAMID OF DIAMONDS

Are the rhombuses on the top of this pyramid lighter than those on the bottom?

No, they are identical. Compare the points! The color gradation being on a surface that gets more and more narrow is what creates this illusion.

DONKEY BONNET

Do you see the bird hiding in this image by Épinal?

L'Ane et l'Oiseau

It's hiding in the donkey's ears, which form the bird's wings!

BALANCING

Are these people playing on a teeter-totter?

In this snapshot, the people seem to each be resting on the extremities of a teeter-totter. Obviously, this is not the case. The effect is caused by a confusion of the different planes. The photo flattens the depth, making the people and the bar appear to be in the same plane.

DOTS AND LINES

Are these
dots aligned?

Yes they are, but the position of the lines produces an angled effect that distorts our perception of the alignment. The dots seem to follow the orientation of the lines, which creates a visual discrepancy.

LITTLE DIAMONDS

Which of these four diamond shapes is the lightest?

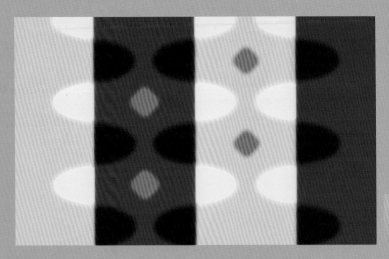

None. The two diamonds on the right appear darker than those to the left because the background is lighter.

THE INFERNAL TOWER

Is the ground shaking?

This strange, wavy tower is actually the reflection of a real building on the glass sides of another. Look at the left part of the photo, and you'll see a piece of a real crane (in red).

IN THE NAVY

What are these three sailors holding?

At first glance, they appear to each be holding a bayonet in their right hand. But in reality, there is a discrepancy at the center of the image: the top and bottom parts don't match. The alternating of the open and closed outlines creates this ambiguity.

A STRANGE CIRCLE

What do you notice
when you observe
this circle?

It seems deformed, but if you
colored this circle in, you would
see that it's perfectly round.
The three series of yellow lines
disturb your vision to the extent
that the left part of the circle
appears to be slightly flattened.

CROSS-HATCHING

Are the red lines in all the squares the same shade?

Yes, although they appear darker in the squares where they're next to purple lines than they do in those where they're next to orange lines. The neighboring colors affect our perception.

A READING GAME

Can you understand this text?

Toam saivd to himrself thact it wzas not suvch a hofllow wordld, aftwer all. He had discovgered a greawt laew of hujman acytion, wituhout knbowing it — namlely, thaot in orbder to mauke a maqn or a boy cotvet a thaing, it is onbly necetssary to maike the thding diffiscult to atteain.

Excerpt from *Tom Sawyer* by Mark Twain

Despite the additional letters in the passage from this novel, our brain reconstitutes the original text without difficulty because of our extensive reading experience. We recognize known words by skipping the superfluous characters.

A FISHERMAN WITHOUT FISH

"Where is my fish?"

The fish is hiding in the tree, vertically, between the branches.

A PACIFIST UTOPIA

Do you see a steering wheel or a peace symbol?

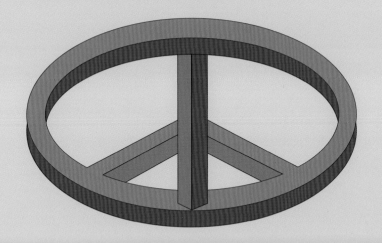

Such a steering wheel would not be very useful! This object is not reproducible in 3-D. The representation of its height, created by the shadows cast, produce an inconsistent perspective. If we consider it in 2-D, we see a flat peace symbol.

MEMORIES OF A GOLDFISH

Stare at the image on the left for a few seconds and then move your eyes to the one on the right. What do you notice?

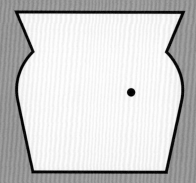

A goldfish appears! Our visual receptors are saturated after staring at the white shape on the red background. Through retinal persistence, when you look at the white surface you see the residual image of the fish appear in red, with a white eye and a black pupil at its center.

THE SOUL OF THE TOWER

Who is the main character in this photo?

Initially, you probably noticed the central silhouette holding the umbrella, but by observing the image as a whole, you will see a second person: the face of a person whose forehead is created by the arc of the Eiffel Tower and whose face is contoured by the shadows on the ground. The person with the umbrella and his shadow outline the nose, and the trees in the background form the eyes.

RED LINES

Which red line is longer?

They are identical, although the one in the back appears longer because the lines on the road distort our perception of the lengths. To convince yourself, measure them with a ruler.

AND THERE WAS LIGHT...

Stare at the lightbulb for 30 seconds then stare at the white background. What happens?

The lightbulb turns on! It's a residual image created by the stimulation of your retinal photoreceptors. The misinterpretation doesn't happen in your brain but rather in your eyes.

SMALL SQUARES

Are the squares
properly aligned
in this image?

Yes they are, but the
alternation of the orange and
red shapes as well as the
slight misalignment of the
interior squares create the
illusion of a distortion of the
vertical and horizontal lines.

SUMMER FLOWERS

Stare at this image for around 10 seconds. What do you see?

The flowers gradually start to spin, yet nothing is actually moving! The position of the colors and the light and dark areas create an imaginary movement.

DOUBLE DIAMONDS

Can this drawing be
reproduced in 3-D?

No. It's an impossible object
since the bars superimpose
themselves while occupying
the same spatial plane. To be
realistic, the drawing should
show, in perspective, the
overlapping of the elements.

RADIOACTIVE

Is the center
of this image
whiter
than the
background?

No. We think we see an
illuminated dot in the center
of the figure, but it's really the
image's white background. The
gray fading out into the center
of the three triangles and the
contrast with the center creates
the illusion.

THE SKY IS FALLING!

Is this image a photomontage?

No. The sky is reflected in the pavement, which is covered with water. The reflection isn't deformed since the ground is perfectly flat.

ALPHABET

Is it possible to sculpt these letters?

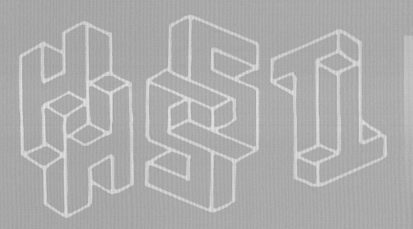

No. They can only exist as a drawing. We can clearly distinguish the "H," "S" and "T," but staring at each form disturbs our vision, since each appears to be made up of two letters. In fact, the letters share ambiguous outlines, and their spatial orientation appears to change when we try to interpret them in perspective. We can only look at one letter at a time, yet we see both.

TWIN TRIANGLES

Which triangle is darker?

They are both the same shade of pink. The arrangement of the shapes and their colors alter your perception. The triangle on the left looks lighter because of the purple background. The triangle on the right, which is turned at 90 degrees, looks darker because it's on the green background.

WATCH OUT, IT'S SHINY!

Stare at the yellow circle. What do you see?

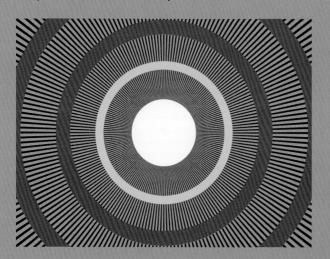

White spots seem to be spinning inside the blue circles. This illusion is created by the contrast between the black and white lines.

PINK BARS

Which pink bar is longer?

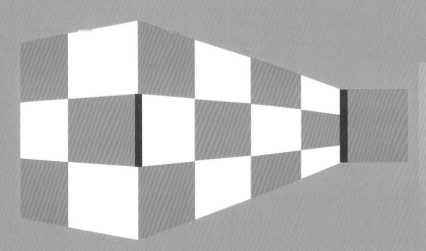

They are the same length, but the bar on the left looks shorter than the one on the right. This illusion is created by an effect of perspective and also by the checkerboard. We estimate the size of the bars in relation to the squares; those on the right are smaller, which, by contrast, makes the bar look bigger.

IMPAIRED LINES

Are the red lines straight?

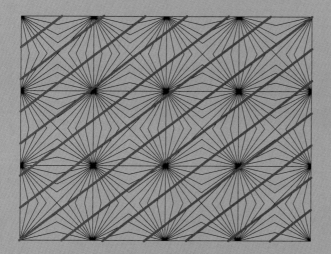

They are perfectly straight and parallel to one another. The black lines of the pattern in the background force your eyes to concentrate on the circles, which distorts your perception of the red lines, making them look curvy.

ARMISTICE

Who appears in this drawing?

Upright, we see a French soldier from the First World War. If you turn the image upside down, however, the profile of a German soldier with a mustache appears.

MAZE

What does this drawing represent?

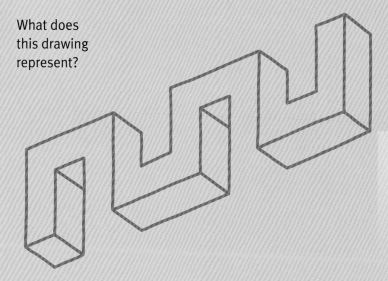

If you look at the top of the drawing, you see two slots and two more on the bottom. However, if you try to look at the image as a whole it becomes incoherent, since none of the slots is actually closed; the outlines are ambiguous. This is an impossible object, and our perception of it requires displacing the optical reference point.

341

CUBOID

This object cannot
actually exist.
Why?

Because the assemblage
of lines in the middle of
the cube contains junctures
with edges that are totally
incompatible with the
laws of perspective. These
lines sometimes look like
they're inside the cube, and
sometimes they look like
they're on the outside of it.

CHECKERS!

Is the white square in the middle of this checkerboard brighter than the others?

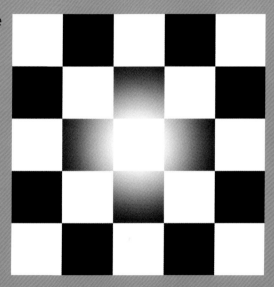

It looks brighter, but it's only an optical effect. The fading gray color in the four black squares around it create the illusion, provoking a strong surface contrast.

WAVES

What happens when you look at the yellow and green curves?

They seem to shine! Essentially, the green spots appear to move laterally along the yellow background. The human eye tires quickly when we focus on an object. By moving your gaze around the image, you are putting the different persistent images in conflict, which creates the illusion of movement.

A LIGHTER SHADE OF GREEN?

Are the diagonal lines the same shade of green throughout this image?

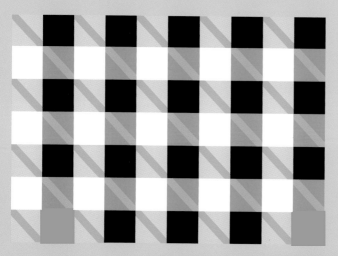

They are, but your eyes, influenced by the changing background of the checkerboard, perceive a lighter shade of green when the diagonal lines intersect a dark square and a darker shade of green against the light squares.

HEXAGON

Is this hexagon regular?

Yes it is, but the triangles interfere with our perception of it. We have the impression that they are masking an approximate figure.

MAJESTIC LIKE AN EAGLE

Which animal is the darker of the two?

They are the same color, but the background colors influence our perception, making the eagle on the top seem darker. The brain distinguishes colors in relation to the environment, and the fading effect reinforces the illusion by contrasting the light background against the dark background.

LABYRINTH

What does this drawing represent?

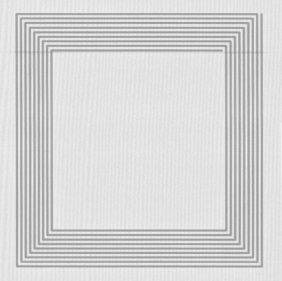

It is not a series of embedded squares, as you might believe at first glance. Up close, you can see that the drawing is made up of one single continuous line that ends at the inside right of the central square and in the right angle in the exterior of the drawing.

END POINT?

Cross the island by following the single line to the left. What will be your end point, the yellow line or the red line?

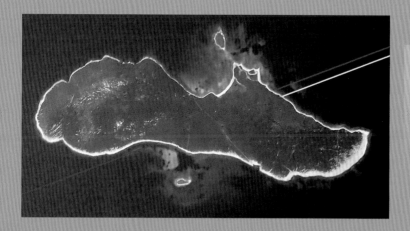

You likely have no doubt that the two red lines are continuous, but the end point is actually the yellow line. This is called the Poggendorff illusion and is named after the physician who discovered it in 1860. The eye struggles to interpret linearity when an obstacle breaks the continuity of a line.

ROSETTES

Do you see concentric circles in this image?

We think we see a series of circles, but they don't actually exist. The illusion is due to the lighter points that appear where the rosettes intersect, which are the result of the brightness contrast between the pink and white backgrounds.

THE GHOST OF NAPOLEON

Centuries after the death of Napoleon on the island of St. Helena, his spirit still seems to inhabit the surroundings. Do you see him?

He is standing between the two tree trunks on the left, with his body slightly turned.

ON A BICYCLE

Look intently at the bike's wheels. What happens?

They start to turn! The alternating black and white circles, which are very close together, and our knowledge of the movement of the wheels of a bike create the illusion.

CIRCLES IN MOTION

What do you
see when
you stare at
the dot in the
center of this
image?

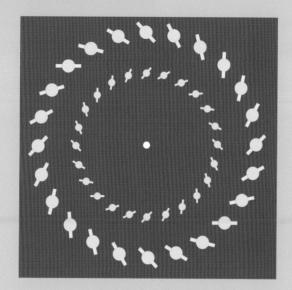

The two circles look like
they're spinning in opposite
directions. This illusion plays
with our peripheral vision,
and the small yellow lines
create the effect. These lines
are oriented in two different
directions, and they make our
gaze "slide" in the direction
in which they're oriented.

DEW DROPS

Scan the image with your eyes and observe the round patterns. What happens?

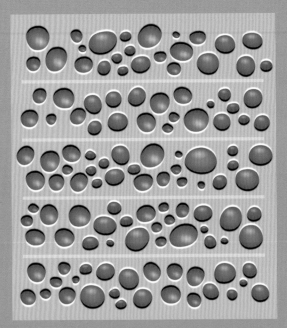

The "dew drops" seem to be moving and rippling. This illusion rests on the interplay between the colors used: the black and white outlines appear to cast shadows, which give height to the patterns and make them look like they're repelling one another. The yellow horizontal lines reinforce this effect by orienting the direction of our perception of the drops.

A CURSORY GLANCE

Are the eyes of this person aligned?

Yes they are, even though the holes in the black band give us the impression that they're lopsided. We see a discrepancy because of the strong contrast between the light and dark backgrounds, which tricks our brain.

GHOST DOTS

Do you see little white dots moving up and down the blue lines?

These dots don't exist. The contrast in the brightness of the black and white patterns around the blue bands creates the illusion of the white dots.

RUNNING WATER

Stare at the dark bands between the streams of water. What do you see?

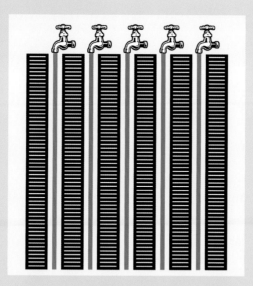

The water looks like it's running! This effect of imaginary movement is created by the gray on the striped bands as well as the alternating vertical and horizontal directions. The contrast between the light and dark colors reinforces the illusion.

THE TRAMP

Look at this portrait and then stare at a white surface. Whom do you recognize?

Charlie Chaplin appears as a residual image!

CURVES

Which pair of figures has the biggest curve?

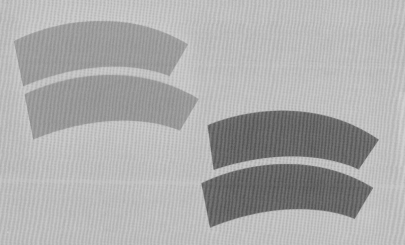

They are identical! In the blue pair, the left sides are collinear (aligned), which gives the impression that they are of different sizes. In the purple pair, the right upper corners are on a vertical line, which makes the optical effect disappear. This illusion is called the Jastrow illusion.

ARC DE TRIOMPHE

Could you build such a structure?

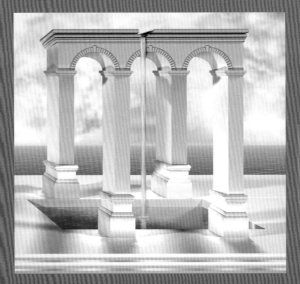

When we look at the top of this arch, the four columns look aligned. However, at the bottom of the drawing, they seem to be straddling the pool. This double perspective creates the illusion of multiple surfaces and, as a result, an impossible construction.

THREE ROLLERS

Do you see the movement of the rollers in this image?

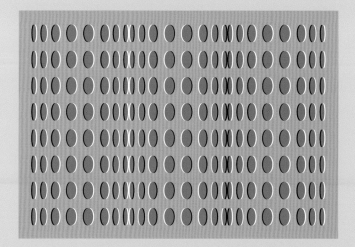

This is the work of Akiyoshi Kitaoka, a master in the art of optical illusions. Here, the lines of the more or less narrow ovals simulate volume seen from different angles, which generates the impression of depth, creating the illusion of a surface of moving rollers.

AN OCEAN OF WORDS

What are you reading?

The ywear 1866 was marfked by a bizawrre develfop-
ment, an unexqplained and dowdnright inexpclicable
phenonmenon that suarely no one has forgvotten.
Withoudt geotting into those ruamors that updset
civilioans in the seawports and deravnged the pubrlic
mirnd even far inltand, it must be saied that pro-
fessnional seaqmen were espercially alarwmed.

Excerpt from *20,000 Leagues Under the Sea* by Jules Verne

Despite the additional letters,
we manage to read this
excerpt. In the same way we
decode a foreign language,
we lean on the context and
our lexical knowledge to
re-form words so the text
makes sense.

CONJOINED TWINS?

Which woman is facing the camera?

It's impossible to know! This puzzling photo makes us wonder, but this face could belong to either woman.

CHECKMATE

What color are the dots at the angles of the squares?

We think we see three different shades of gray, but the dots are all the same shade! The areas of light and shadow on the board skew our perception. The gray appears darker on the light background and lighter on the dark background. The contrast is stronger due to the dots' small size in relation to the surface of the squares.

WHEN THE CAT'S AWAY...

How many animals
do you see in this
drawing?

The cat is easy to see, but
looking more closely at the
face, you can see a mouse;
the eyes of the cat form its
ears, the nostrils its eyes
and both share the teeth
and whiskers.

ABSTRACT ART

What do you
see in these
black and white
shapes?

By observing the top right
side of the drawing, you'll
see the face of a bearded
man appear!

FROM BOTTOM TO TOP

Which pattern do you first see in this drawing?

The colored images transform themselves alternately from background to shapes that make sense. If we stare at the blue background, we see arrowheads; however, when we look at the red background, a line of little men in profile seems to be going down stairs.

SIMILARITIES AND DIFFERENCES

Place a pencil between each band of color. What do you notice?

The bands seem to be the same color! This is called the Chevreul illusion and is named for the 19th century French chemist who put forward the theory of simultaneous contrast. According to this theory, two zones of the same color that are unevenly darkened will influence one another when they are next to each other; the eye, deceived, modifies the intensity of the color.

AN INFINITE DOME

Is this architecture real?

It is actually a good example of an architectural trompe l'oeil. The patterns on the walls of the dome create an effect of depth, when in reality it is only a painting. The vanishing point of the circle in the middle, which is very light, attracts the eye. In addition, the area of light painted on the bottom left amplifies the impression of depth.

SWIMMING PROHIBITED

These two rascals think they can swim, but a police officer is watching. Can you see him?

His silhouette is drawn in the sky between the two tree trunks.

INDEX